Access in Mind

towards the inclusive museum

Ann Rayner

The Intellectual Access Trust

This project would not have been possible without the unstinting encouragement, advice and practical and financial help of a great number of individuals and organisations. They are too many to list in full, and it is invidious to select, but it would be discourteous not to mention at least some. The Trustees of INTACT and the Project Officer would therefore like to thank most sincerely:–

The Patrons of INTACT who are listed on a separate page and whose willingness to lend their names to the project gave it credibility, not least in fund-raising.

The organisations who helped us financially and who are listed separately inside the back cover. Our almost literal debt to them is real and immense, and we hope that the result, in this report and other work including the post-project training seminars, will justify their confidence in us.

The members of the Steering Committee, listed on a separate page.

The Hon Auditor, who gave his professional services free of charge.

The Director and staff of the National Museums of Scotland, who provided the Project Officer with an office base; who gave professional personnel and financial services cover for her employment from the recruitment process onwards; whose Head of Public Affairs acted as line manager; and whose Disability Liaison Officer, Education officers, curators, designers, multimedia and publications staff all contributed with their differing expertise. Their support, too, has been crucial and has greatly reduced our overhead costs so that virtually every penny we raised has gone directly into productive project work.

The Director and staff of the Scottish Museums Council, who gave access to their library; whose Training Manager arranged the post-project programme of training seminars in Scotland; and who will manage a post-project monitoring survey.

Alison Coles, Access Co-ordinator, Museums and Galleries Commission.

David Anderson, Head of Education at the Victoria and Albert Museum.

The Directors and staff of the many museums and galleries who gave help and advice, some of whom are listed separately as partners in pilot projects.

Members of the Museums and Galleries Disability Association (MAGDA) or the Group for Education in Museums (GEM), who include: Margaret Bowden, Jem Fraser, William Kirby, Sandra Marwick, Gillian Mason, Stephanie McIver, Sue Picton, Gill Poulter, Maria Regan, Pat Reynolds, Sarah Scaife, Helen Sinclair and Anne Tynan.

Dr. Jan Walmsley, School of Health and Social Welfare, the Open University.

The Director and staff of Historic Scotland, and especially those who helped with the Jedburgh Project.

Staff of the White Top Research Unit of Dundee University and the Profound and Multiple Impairment Service (PAMIS).

Dr. Uist MacDonald of Ceres Computer Consultants; Heather Jack of KeyComm; Paul Nisbet and others at the Edinburgh University CALL Centre; Wyness Glennie and Michael Marrick of Capability Scotland; and Ivan Mykytyn of the Scottish Council for Educational Technology for advice on computers and switchgear. (Do not contemplate a computer interactive installation unless you have a computer expert such as Dr. MacDonald on board!).

Alison Wilkie of Albavision, Inverness (and her husband who carried the tripod!).

Shona McMillan and her colleagues in A.C.T. (Arts Communication and Technology, now Antenna).

James Carter, consultant and trainer in interpretation; Julie Forrest of Scottish Natural Heritage; and Dr. Gordon Adams, Director of Planning and Development at the Scottish Tourist Board, who all gave advice on interpretation.

Staff at the Fruitmarket Gallery, Edinburgh; the Contact Gallery, Edinburgh; and Project Ability Centre for Developmental Art, Glasgow.

The Training Officer, David Douglas, and tenants of Key Housing, Glasgow, and especially the stars of the video 'Get the Picture'.

Staff and students from the special needs departments at Jewel & Esk Valley, Stevenson and Telford Colleges of Further Education.

Staff and users from the many day and resource centres who took part in pilot projects and helped with suggestions and feedback.

Members of People First and local co-ordinators in Edinburgh and the Borders.

Other individuals, including:– Alasdair Hutton, the "Voice of the Tattoo"; Dr Lesley Glasser of Satrosphere; Babs McCool, of Art in Partnership; Dr Ian Newman, Phil Chambers and Graham Attridge of the Fieldfare Trust; Brian Perrett and Henry Gray of BT; Valerie Wardlaw for help with projects (especially *Design your own Tartan*); Moira Blackie for her contribution as volunteer assistant to the Project Officer; Dick and Sheila Burtles; Nick Lowe; Sir John Cox; Sir Alistair Grant; Simon Willoughby-Booth, Head of Art Therapy at Gogarburn Hospital; Alastair Ramage, Curator at the Heatherbank Museum of Social Work; Sue Pirnie of the Scottish Arts Council; Dr Jon Oberlander of Edinburgh University's Department of Artificial Intelligence; Andrew Cunningham.

While our grateful and most sincere thanks are due to all of the above for their help, support, encouragement, co-operation and advice, they are not, of course, responsible for any errors of commission or omission in this report, whose content remains the sole responsibility of the Trustees and the author.

The Intellectual Access Trust (INTACT) was established in 1995 to raise awareness of the social, educational, cultural and economic importance of making displays in museums, galleries and historic properties more accessible to people with learning or communication disabilities.

We were fairly surprised to learn that less than 5% of people with disabilities are wheelchair users, but very surprised to discover the statistics in respect of intellectual disability: there are a million people with learning disabilities and seven million adults with literacy problems. Add to that the number of their accompanying relatives, friends, carers or teachers and that's an enormous number of visitors for whom a trip around a museum is a real challenge.

With the introduction of the Disability Discrimination Act there is now not only a moral duty but a statutory one to provide for these significant numbers. INTACT believed that while issues of physical and sensory access are beginning to be actively addressed in public buildings, awareness of the importance of intellectual access was barely off the starting blocks.

In setting up its two-year research project, INTACT's key objectives were:

- to study what work had been done already, whether published or not, and to gather it together in order to draw attention to it

- to carry out a number of pilot projects on possible means of improving access

- to set out some conclusions and offer guidelines for action

- and to motivate governing bodies and staff of museums and galleries to think how the emerging ideas might be applied and further developed in the context of their own, widely different displays

The intention of this report is to produce some research and guidance which would move museums towards a more inclusive approach. We hope that what you will find is some stimulation to broaden access to existing and potential user groups in museums, galleries and historic properties because embracing the principles in this report will result in a better communicated message to **all** visitors.

The Minister for the Arts in Scotland published in March 1998 a draft code of good practice on access to museums and galleries. The Trustees of INTACT were delighted to see a government paper which specifically acknowledges the need to provide intellectual as well as physical and sensory access. We have sent comments on this draft to Scottish Office and we very much hope that some of the content of this report will be built into the final version of the Code.

Our Project Officer, Ann Rayner, has done a most commendable job in researching and compiling this publication and for this the Trustees of INTACT are very grateful. Many other acknowledgments to those bodies and individuals who believed in us are found elsewhere in the text. However, a special mention must be made of one other individual whose vision it was to establish INTACT and whose tireless and heroic fund raising meant that the research project, the training seminars and this final publication have come to fruition. To Ronnie Cramond, the Secretary and driving force behind INTACT must go all our thanks.

Rosi Capper
Convener
INTACT

AAM	American Association of Museums
ACT	Arts Communication and Technology
CAF	Charities Aid Foundation
CALL Centre	Communication Aids for Language and Learning Centre
DAT	Digital Audio Tape
DCMS	Department for Culture, Media and Sport
DDA	Disability Discrimination Act
DNH	Department of National Heritage
EISF	Edinburgh International Science Festival
FAIR	Family Advice and Information Resource
FE	Further Education
GEM	Group for Education in Museums
HMSO	Her Majesty's Stationery Office
ICOM	International Council of Museums
Ilex	Intelligent Label Explorer
INTACT	Intellectual Access Trust
JEM	Journal for Education in Museums
MAGDA	Museums and Galleries Disability Association
MGC	Museums and Galleries Commission
MHF	Mental Health Foundation
MOSAICS	Museum of Scotland Advanced Interactive Computer System
MTI	Museum Training Institute
NIACE	National Institute of Adult Continuing Education
NGS	National Galleries of Scotland; these consist of the National Gallery of Scotland, the Scottish National Portrait Gallery and the Scottish National Gallery of Modern Art
NMS	National Museums of Scotland; these include the Royal Museum and the Museum of Scotland which opens in November 1998
N/SVQ	National/Scottish Vocational Qualification
NTS	National Trust for Scotland
PAMIS	Profound and Multiple Impairment Service
PMLD	Profound and Multiple Learning Difficulties
RMS	Royal Museum of Scotland
RNIB	Royal National Institute for the Blind
RNID	Royal National Institute for the Deaf
ROM	Royal Ontario Museum
SAC	Scottish Arts Council
SCRAN	Scottish Cultural Resources Access Network
SDSA	Scottish Down's Syndrome Association
SHIRLIE	Support, Help, Initiative, Recreation, Leisure, Independence and Education
SMC	Scottish Museums Council
SNH	Scottish Natural Heritage
SOEID	Scottish Office Education and Industry Department
STB	Scottish Tourist Board
UNESCO	United Nations Educational, Scientific and Cultural Organisation

Before starting as INTACT Project Officer in May 1996, I had been aware of the limited choice of activities and opportunities for people with learning or communication disabilities. Enjoying visits to museums and galleries myself, I sometimes took the young people I worked with to such places to introduce them to new experiences, either during holidays or as an occasional leisure activity.

These visits were often extremely frustrating. We had usually chosen to visit a particular place because of the subject matter, having seen a leaflet or poster, or having been told about it. However, it was disappointing to find how little there often was for people with learning disabilities if the displays consisted of objects behind glass and only written information to explain what they were.

Because of problems of mobility, vision, inability to read or lack of a cultural vocabulary, these people were dependent on those who accompanied them, such as myself, not just to read information to them, but very often to explain it as well. What they got was a 'second hand' experience. Unless they were very assertive, even this choice as to what was explained to them tended to be limited to what the companion chose to share with them.

Where an effort had been made to provide hands-on experiences, where visitors could listen to information on audio or hear sounds which made a static display come alive, where there were working machines (even models or video film), or where there were museum staff or volunteers to talk about the displays, these young people thoroughly enjoyed this widening of their horizons and would remember the experience and talk about it. Such exhibitions were all the more appreciated because of their rarity but the fact that we came across them now and again encouraged us to persevere with museum visiting.

It was efforts like these few outstanding examples that suggested that museums, galleries and historic buildings could provide better access to their displays if such examples of good practice could be made more widely known. This, coupled with the belief that people with learning disabilities do not get a good deal in society because of their problems in making their voices heard, has governed my attitude to this project.

The skills and interests of people with learning disabilities are often under-rated because they are unrecognised. A young man I know has an amazing sense of direction. He has only to travel a route once, whether by bus, car or on foot, to be able to follow it perfectly, even in reverse. When his father could not find the family car in a large car park, it was his 'learning disabled' son who was able to go straight to it. In other words his spatial intelligence was highly developed.

Equally people can find interest and enjoyment in areas others might not suspect. I have known a teenage boy who loved Mozart, listening to classical music from choice, and an elderly woman who liked surrealist art. Both had learning disabilities, but had been fortunate enough to discover these interests. Had they not, they would have missed a great deal of stimulation and pleasure.

In a similar way, visiting museums and galleries can inspire new interests or develop those already existing. The need for some research into access to museums and galleries for people with learning disabilities and to bring together ideas and examples of good practice was identified by Anne Pearson in her paper *Museum Education*

It was disappointing to find how little there often was for people with learning disabilities if the displays consisted of objects behind glass and only written information to explain what they were.

and Disability which appears in *Initiatives in Museum Education*, edited by Eilean Hooper-Greenhill (1989). She said that while some museums, for example the Horniman in London, have developed excellent services for people with learning disabilities:

> it is impossible to estimate the extent and quality of provision nationally because those involved are usually dealing as best they can with particular groups and have no time to reflect on their work or write up their experience. There is a crying need for an exchange of ideas and experience in this aspect of Museum Education.

This need was recognised by the Trustees of INTACT who hope that this research and publication go some way to bridge the gap. I am very grateful indeed to the INTACT Trustees for making this possible by funding the project and for allowing me to combine so many interests in working on it.

Ann Rayner

People with learning difficulties are often their own best ambassadors; the best education is actually to meet a real person. Conversely, it is very difficult to inform people or to change their views unless they have that opportunity.
R McConkey, *Who Cares? Community Involvement with Handicapped People* London (1987).

Background

INTACT, the Intellectual Access Trust, was set up with the express purpose of improving access to museums, galleries and historic sites for people with learning and communication disabilities. The thinking behind this was set out in a paper published in the *Times Educational Supplement Scotland* of 3 May 1996. Copies were then sent to many organisations and contacts to introduce INTACT's aims and objectives.

The paper proposed a two year research project, for which the work programme was:

1. to study all existing work on intellectual access

2. to survey existing displays with curators, education staff, guides, designers and security staff (who see where different groups of visitors already go) to identify candidates for pilot projects

3. with the co-operation of staff of schools, adult training and resource centres and caring bodies, and with advice on and reactions to access directly from people with learning disabilities, to discuss and observe needs. Then to devise and arrange a series of visits both by individuals and by small groups of persons with a range of learning disabilities

4. to identify which exhibits excite interest and how that interest could be increased by interactive and other educational or communication techniques such as supplying suitable handling material

5. to set up and monitor a number of pilot projects to look at ways of improving museum provision for people with learning disabilities

6. to explore the scope for developing audio guides to cater more specifically for those with reading impairment or other communication difficulty

7. to draw conclusions, write up results and make recommendations for future provision

8. to devise and implement training seminars for museum staff and volunteer guides in museums throughout Scotland and the UK

Making access easier for those with learning disabilities will actually help a much greater section of the population, including those with sight problems (some resulting from ageing), the 7.3 million adults with literacy problems[1] and those whose first language is not English. Dr Jan Walmsley of the Open University's School of Health and Social Welfare, who was consulted when the project was being set up, emphasised this element. George Hein in *Evaluating a Display adapted for People with Learning Difficulties*, concludes:

By instituting changes intended to make an exhibition more accessible to a special population, the museum made it more accessible to all. By expanding accessibility we increase both the enjoyment and the potential for learning for all our visitors.[2]

Making museums more welcoming to a wider audience is a recurring theme of this

Making museums more welcoming to a wider audience is a recurring theme of this report. If making them more friendly for those with learning disabilities helps to achieve this, then the work of INTACT has wider relevance than might at first appear.

The DDA presents museums with new challenges, but also gives them the chance to reconsider the meaning and importance of access to collections. [4]

report. If making them more friendly for those with learning disabilities helps to achieve this, then the work of INTACT has wider relevance than might at first appear.

There are a great many people who visit museums rarely, if ever. The reasons given for this include the belief that museums are boring, they are only for 'boffins', or they are regarded as places to take the children or grandchildren as a duty because they are 'educational'. A respondent to the survey detailed in *Dingy Places with different kinds of bits*, London Museum Service (1991), described museum visiting:

> you are not getting involved in anything, you are just going and having a look – it gets boring for a child … it is difficult to stimulate the mind when you are just looking at still objects all the time and reading the cards. [3]

This survey found that the people questioned liked displays that involved the onlooker, such as working models and hands-on opportunities.

Many highly intelligent people with dyslexia and many elderly people with deteriorating eyesight would not regard themselves as disabled. But they would probably prefer less written information about displays than is commonly presented or, at least, a hierarchy of text which allows them to read as little as they want and still get the main message. If the normal displays are made as accessible as possible to the widest range of people with or without disabilities, then this helps everyone.

Traditionally the range of objects displayed in museums and the way in which they have been interpreted has been, with some exceptions, from a white, western, middle-class, well-educated, predominantly male, perspective. This places huge barriers to intellectual access in front of a large section of the population and gives them the impression that museums are not for them. It is hardly surprising that they react by dismissing museums as boring or having an intimidating atmosphere.

Yet, if we believe that museums are a 'good thing' because they tell people about:

- their own history which gives them a sense of identity
- other cultures which can widen their perspective
- the natural world, discoveries in science and engineering, the oldest rocks and what lives in the deepest oceans
- and let them see original works of art from different periods and cultures

then, if we believe that public money should be used to support them, we cannot deny access to any group on the grounds of physical, sensory or intellectual differences any more than we can on the grounds of race, religion or sex.

Under the Disability Discrimination Act of 1995, museums are legally obliged to make their services, and eventually their buildings, accessible to people with disabilities. As Rebecca McGinnis points out:

> The DDA presents museums with new challenges, but also gives them the chance to reconsider the meaning and importance of access to collections. [4]

It might be argued that people with learning disabilities who have limited understanding may not be able to appreciate what museums and galleries have to offer. However, just as no-one is expected to read all the books in a library, no-one is expected to look at all the objects in a museum, far less read all the labels. People with learning disabilities, like everyone else, appreciate being able to browse, to look at what is on display and to stop and find out more about the things which catch their attention. If they do not know what is available, they cannot know what might capture their interest.

Too often, the rest of us make assumptions about what people with learning disabilities like, or how they might wish to spend their time. In fact museums are potentially very suitable places for them, and for others who may have poor literacy skills, to broaden their experience and learn about history, science or art. Museums use objects rather than books to convey their messages. The learner is able to proceed at his/her own pace, to identify things s/he is interested in and to investigate further where this interest is aroused.

Objects, potentially, can be made accessible to everyone. This can be done by displaying them in a context such as a room setting for domestic objects, a diorama for natural history specimens, relating old or unfamiliar objects to contemporary, familiar equivalents, or showing by means of maps where objects have been found . It can be done by provoking questions: what is this made of? who made it? why? where did it come from? who used it? They can also stimulate the emotions, and provide material for art and drama which in turn can help to develop insight. Objects, particularly those that can be handled, are a focus for the memory, aiding the recall of facts and ideas. They are a direct link with the past or with other cultures.

By working with real things, making comparisons, remembering, making relationships, interrogating, moving from concrete observations to abstract concepts, moving from specific observations to generalisations, extending from the known to the unknown, following the pace and the interests of the learner, true cognitive and emotional processes may take place that lead to changed perceptions and the growth of new ideas.[5]

This quotation from J. Henniger-Shuh, *Teaching yourself to teach with objects* is as true for those with learning disabilities as it is for anyone else.

As it is impossible to draw strict divisions between those who have learning disabilities and those who do not, it is divisive to make special programmes the only provision for a particular group. However, there may be circumstances where special arrangements may be appropriate in addition to what is provided for the general public.

... just as no-one is expected to read all the books in a library, no-one is expected to look at all the objects in a museum, far less read all the labels.

Learning and Communication Disabilities

Learning or communication disabilities are usually the result of an impairment in brain function which may have been inherited, acquired during the perinatal period, or acquired as the result of an illness or trauma during the early years of life. They are not something which can be treated or 'cured', nor can they be caught.

People with learning disabilities, along with those with mental health problems, are particularly disadvantaged. To many, the idea of disability conjures up a mental picture of a wheelchair or possibly a guide dog, and too often institutions feel that they have addressed the issue by installing a ramp and a toilet with a wide door and a grab-rail.

People with physical and sensory impairments have a much higher profile than people with intellectual impairments as they

Those with learning and communication disabilities are often, by the very nature of their disabilities, unable to speak for themselves and thus have to rely on others to do this for them.

Everyone has their own particular intelligence profile with which they are born, and which will change during life according to the person's opportunities and experiences.

are more able to speak for themselves and make the public aware of the discrimination they face. Increasingly they are doing just that, and are insisting on speaking out for themselves and asking for what they feel are their rights rather than being made to feel the recipients of charity.

Those with learning and communication disabilities are often, by the very nature of their disabilities, unable to speak for themselves and thus have to rely on others to do this for them. This situation is beginning to change with the growth of organisations like *'People First'* or *'Values into Action'* which are trying to give a voice to people with learning disabilities. However, even here there is a danger that members of these organisations, who are effectively the more articulate, may not be able to represent fully the concerns of those who are more severely impaired.

There is a special discrimination against people with intellectual impairments who are often seen as the 'less deserving'. Charities set up to help them tend to get less money[6] than those to help people with other disabilities. People with other disabilities often find it necessary to emphasise that they are not mentally impaired, as if this were peculiarly humiliating. Words like 'mental' or 'spastic' have become used as insults so that organisations which help those with learning or communication disabilities have changed their names in recent years; the Scottish Society for the Mentally Handicapped has become Enable and the Scottish Council for Spastics has become Capability Scotland.

Sarah Scaife in *Welcoming Adults with Learning Disabilities at Wakefield Museums and Galleries* mentions the problems of people who are still isolated and shunned by mainstream society and suggests that one of the biggest hurdles in working with them is the fear experienced by museum staff who have never met anyone with a learning disability.

Supporting front of house staff through training is important if adults with learning disabilities are to feel more welcome in our building.[7]

She points out that few museum educators know about the educational development of people with learning disabilities, who until the 1971 Act of Parliament were considered 'ineducable'. Some of the adults visiting museums now may be unable to read because they were never taught to do so.

Our preoccupation with intelligence, whatever that is, as a measure for valuing people is very limiting. Alfred Binet[8] defined intelligence as *"what my test serves to measure"*. The American, Howard Gardner, in *Frames of Mind*,[9] suggests that there are roughly seven types of intelligence: linguistic, logical-mathematical, spatial, bodily-kinaesthetic, musical, interpersonal and intrapersonal. He suggests that we put the first two of these on a pedestal and give them an exaggerated importance, whereas all types should be thought of as equally important. Everyone has their own particular intelligence profile with which they are born, and which will change during life according to the person's opportunities and experiences.

Qualities such as generosity and thoughtfulness, accepting people and situations as they are without trying to change them, taking pleasure in simple things like food, sunshine, the sound of running water, and showing feelings naturally rather than covering them up are not highly valued in our market-led society. While not all of those with learning disabilities demonstrate these qualities, many of them can help the rest of us to appreciate an alternative way of looking at things and this is of value in itself.

This was recognised by Jean Vannier, the founder of L'Arche, who created communities in several countries where people with learning disabilities can live alongside 'so-called normal people'. In *The Challenge of L'Arche*, he says;

> Handicapped people, particularly those who are less able, are frequently endowed with qualities of heart which serve to remind so-called normal people that their own hearts are closed. Their simplicity frequently serves to reveal our duplicity, untruthfulness and hypocrisy. Their acceptance of their own situation and their humility frequently reveals our pride and our refusal to accept others as they are.[10]

People with learning or communication disabilities are a heterogeneous group and the degree to which they may be affected can vary tremendously. Among those labelled as having learning disabilities only a very small proportion are severely or profoundly impaired. Yet many otherwise intelligent people can be heard stating that they are useless at mathematics or spelling or cannot speak a language other than English! If this resulted in their being labelled as having a learning disability, they would be very insulted. Intelligence is relative. Many people with learning disabilities have skills in some areas which are higher than average, such as the well documented abilities of some people with autism in music, mathematics or drawing.

Learning disabilities can arise from a large number of inherited disorders of which the best known is Down's Syndrome. Another significant group results from adverse factors at birth such as trauma or anoxia. A number of infective conditions, before, during or after birth can also can give rise to learning disabilities. In the media in recent years some prominence has been given to well-known people with dyslexia and their struggles, and also to people with autism, the causes of which are still not understood.

Within any category there are enormous variations in the extent of the impairment. Many people with Down's Syndrome learn to read and write and are able to lead independent lives. People with cerebral palsy can have physical problems ranging from very mild to extremely severe (ie having no independent voluntary movement and severe communication problems as a result of this) and may or may not have an additional mental impairment. Sometimes this is suspected or assumed where none exists. People with dyslexia have problems with reading, but may well be of average or above average general intelligence. Those with autism, who have problems in processing information and in communicating and relating to other people, can vary enormously in intelligence or may be particularly gifted in one area such as drawing or mathematics.

People with learning disabilities often have problems in communicating. Severe deafness, whether contracted before or after the acquisition of speech, is not included in this study. However those with speech problems but normal hearing are. These problems may arise from damage to the brain's speech centre, such as caused in a stroke or as an effect of cerebral palsy, or by damage to the organs of speech. Though the circumstances may vary, the fact that a person cannot speak does not by itself mean that s/he does not understand.

Learning disability is one of the most common forms of disability. In the UK over one million people have some form of learning difficulty and about one child in 100 is born with one or develops one while very young.[11] Many people with mild learning disabilities live completely independently and may sometimes be responsible for the

Learning disability is one of the most common forms of disability. In the UK over one million people have some form of learning difficulty and about one child in 100 is born with one or develops one while very young.[11]

The important thing to remember about people with learning disabilities is that they are people, not statistics.

care of others. Of the very small proportion who are regarded as having a severe learning difficulty, the majority live in the community, either with their families or in small residential units with appropriate support. Only around 15,000 adults with learning disabilities in the UK live in hospitals and this number is decreasing all the time as provision is made for even the most severely affected, who may require full time care, to live in the community.

Being labelled as having a learning disability, or indeed any disability, can affect a person's level of education. It is only since the 1971 Act that children with a learning disability were entitled to an education.

The important thing to remember about people with learning disabilities is that they are people, not statistics. They come from all levels of society and all ethnic backgrounds. They are all individuals with widely different interests, likes and dislikes, skills and personality traits, just like everybody else. It is vital to recognise that even if a person cannot speak clearly or has no speech, it does not necessarily mean that he or she cannot understand what you say.

It was decided early in the project to concentrate the research on provision for adults. This is not because learning-disabled children are unimportant, but their needs are better met, in general, than those of adults. Many special schools now are very committed to extending the horizons of their pupils and take them on visits to museums, galleries and historic buildings as part of the curriculum. Also, provision for mainstream children in museums, which is generally of a very high standard where it exists, is often easily adaptable to the needs of pupils with learning disabilities.

Another reason is the need to distance any improvements in provision for adults with learning disabilities from provision for children. While there are a number of common considerations, there are many more differences, and it is important that people with learning disabilities are seen as adults with the status that brings. Finally, the tight time limit on the project made it impossible to explore every area.

Appropriate Terminology

It is no surprise that terminology can be a problem and the changes over the last 20 to 30 years in what is regarded as acceptable are interesting. The profusion of terms used can be a real problem when consulting a book index as they can range from 'feeble-mindedness' to 'cognitive impairment'.

In America in the 1970s, and even into the 1980s, the term 'retarded people' or even 'the retarded' was used, and 'learning disabilities' was restricted to people with dyslexia, auditory perceptual problems or poor short-term memory. Similarly terms like 'the blind', 'the deaf' or 'the disabled' were still found then, though such usage was beginning to be criticised.

In Britain 'mentally handicapped people' was used generally until about the mid 1980s; for example *The Attenborough Report* (1985), *After Attenborough* (1988), and *Arts for Everyone* by Anne Pearson (1985) all use this term. 'Learning difficulties' or 'learning disabilities' has been preferred since the early 1990s. Both *In through the front door* (1992) and *The Big Foot* (1994), use the former term although references to 'the mentally handicapped' appear in quotations. In the USA, 'mentally disabled', 'learning disabled' and 'learning impaired' have all been used relatively recently.

Both 'learning difficulties' and 'learning disabilities' seem to be currently acceptable in Britain. Mencap and Enable refer to people with "learning disabilities" while the Open University and People First, the advocacy organisation, prefer "learning difficulties". This report will use "learning disabilities", except in quotations or when referring to the latest American usage which seems to be moving to "cognitive disabilities" or "cognitive impairment".

Relating to someone with a learning or communication disability

Those who are not accustomed to relating to someone with a learning disability are often unsure how to behave. Anne Tynan in *Adventures in Disability*[12] recognises the embarrassment, unease, fear and guilt often experienced by non-disabled people when they encounter someone with a disability. By looking at the perspectives of both disabled and non-disabled people, she suggests the need for changes in the attitudes and behaviour of both.

The simplest advice about communication with a person who has a learning or communication disability is to speak to him or her as you would to anyone else. Concentrate on the person, not the disability. It is best to keep what you are saying simple and to maintain eye contact so as to know if what you are saying is being understood. Even if the person has a companion, address him or her directly. If there is a problem of understanding, the companion will soon let you know. You may not get a response from the person with the learning disability, but you are more likely to be treated to a beaming smile in recognition of the fact that you did speak to him and acknowledge him as an individual.

Some people, though totally without speech, have excellent inter-personal skills, are very friendly and will show that they want to talk to you or that there is something they want to ask. They will strive to communicate in whatever way they can, whether through a sign language such as Makaton, a Bliss board with words or symbols on it, some form of electronic talker or just by gesture or eye-pointing. Once you establish someone's codes for 'yes' and 'no', which could be as simple as a smile and a frown, it is surprising how far you can go.

Some people with learning or communication disabilities may still be learning about appropriate social behaviour and may be over-friendly or over-talkative. Some may be withdrawn and deliberately avoid eye-contact, while others may make repetitive sounds or gestures. In such situations it is usually best to follow the example of the parents or carers who know the person well. This behaviour may well be caused by unfamiliarity with the situation and could be shortlived.

When one bears in mind the problems that many people with learning disabilities may have through being institutionalised or by experiencing frustration through lack of opportunities for self-expression, such behaviour can be better understood.

Additional and other disabilities

A great deal of the knowledge acquired during this research has been relevant to people with other disabilities. Much of the emphasis on multi-sensory ways of communicating information is applicable to those with sensory impairments. For example, people with sight impairments can be helped by the opportunity to handle objects and by information presented in audio form.

It is not uncommon for a person with a learning disability to have additional

The simplest advice about communication with a person who has a learning or communication disability is to speak to him or her as you would to anyone else. Concentrate on the person, not the disability.

Good intellectual access should be about making information about the objects or works of art on display available to all.

problems which may be sensory or physical. Some may be wheelchair users, or may have some difficulty with balance or with walking any distance. There are thus likely to be references in this report to the needs of people with sensory or physical disabilities alongside the needs of those with learning or communication disabilities.

Museums, Galleries and Historic Sites

The scope of the research was to look initially at access to museums and galleries. To establish what we mean by these terms, here is the Museums Association definition of a museum:

An institution which collects, documents, preserves, exhibits and interprets material evidence and associated information for the public benefit.

This also covers what Americans call an "art museum", a gallery with a permanent collection.

Problems similar to those experienced in museums also occur when people with learning disabilities visit historic sites or buildings. This was recognised by Historic Scotland, who offered INTACT support. In return we have worked with them by running a pilot project at one main site and advising them at others.

It might have been logical to go further down this line and include country or national parks, zoos, safari parks and any visitor attractions where the interpretation of a site, building, animals, local history or natural features is part of the visitor service. However this had to be ruled out because of restraints of time and distance. If some of the ideas and recommendations in this report turn out to be relevant to the needs of those working in such areas, that is a bonus. We are certainly indebted to writers on environmental interpretation, such as Freeman Tilden, John Veverka and James Carter. Their work will be referred to in a later section.

Intellectual Access

What does the Intellectual Access Trust understand by the term 'intellectual access'? The original idea was to look at ways to improve access for people with an intellectual impairment, in the same way that physical access needs to be improved or modified to provide for those with physical disabilities and that alternative means of access should be provided for those with a sensory impairment.

However, just as good physical access helps those with minor mobility problems, as well as wheelchair users, good intellectual access provides information about displays which should help a great many people, not just those who are regarded as having learning disabilities. Information should be provided in a variety of ways and at a number of levels. This will help a wide range of visitors including those with sensory disabilities, people from ethnic minorities, visitors who have limited, or no knowledge of English, people who are not confident readers and ordinary members of the public who would like to visit museums or galleries but may be put off by an unduly academic approach.

Good intellectual access should be about making information about the objects or works of art on display available to all.

The social context in which any learning takes place depends on a variety of basic needs being met first. Abraham Maslow[13] a psychologist, has studied this and has identified a "Hierarchy of Needs" which must be met before people are able to take in information.

Dingy places with different kinds of bits, mentioned earlier[14] refers in section 2.2 to different concepts of access; emotional, physical, political and intellectual. Linking these ideas to those of Maslow's study, which places physiological needs (like not being too hot, cold, tired or needing to use a toilet) at the most basic level, then continues through safety needs, the need to 'belong' and the need for self-esteem to which successful learning contributes, ending with the need for self-actualisation and getting closer to fulfilling our potential, the following hierarchy emerges:

Physical access

This is the most basic. If people cannot get in the door, cannot reach all parts of the building, or are unable to see labels or objects because display cases are the wrong height, they will not be able to appreciate the objects.

Comfortable access

Is it easy for visitors to find their way round? Are there sufficient cafés and restaurants for them to eat and drink when they feel like it? Are there enough seats for visitors to sit, rest and decide what to look at next?

Emotional access

Does the museum environment feel friendly and non-threatening? Are people made to feel welcome and that they have the right to be there? Do displays boost visitors' self-confidence by starting where they are or are they intimidatingly academic in tone?

Personal/social access

Do the displays reflect the social and ethnic mix of the area? Can visitors relate to what they see or, if not, are they helped to do this by the interpretation? Is it easy to see where to go for information, or to find facilities like cafés, lifts and toilets? Does the café sell popular foods and drinks at affordable prices?

Intellectual access

Do displays require prior knowledge of the subject matter? Is the information given by way of a hierarchy so that people with differing levels of knowledge can get what they want? Is this conveyed through a variety of means to accommodate different learning styles, visitors with reading difficulties, or people with a sensory impairment? Can visitors learn at their own pace, make their own connections and set their own agenda? Is it easy for social learning to take place?

The research has shown that easily achieved improvements such as more seating and better signs, or a more imaginative approach to interpretation involving media other than the printed word, can make all the difference to everyone's experience and enjoyment of museums.[16]

The closure of long stay hospitals for the mentally handicapped and mentally ill and the development of community based services gives museums and galleries the opportunity to play an important part in meeting the leisure needs of this section of society.[15]

References

1. Disability Facts and Figures from *The Informability Manual* W Gregory **HMSO** (1997)

2. *Evaluating a Display adapted for People with Learning Difficulties* G Hein *ECSITE* Newsletter Aug/Sept 1990 reproduced in *Developing Museum Exhibitions for Lifelong Learning* edit G Durbin **GEM/Stationery Office** (1996)

3. *Dingy Places with different kinds of bits* **London Museum Service** (1991)

4. *The DDA: duty or opportunity?* R McGinnis **Museum Practice 5** (1997)

5. **Teaching yourself to teach with objects** J Henniger-Shuh quoted in E Hooper-Greenhill's paper *Museums in Education* in *Working with Museums* **SMC** (1988)

6. RNIB 17th, Guide Dogs for the Blind 21st, RNID 36th and MenCap 64th in CAF's list of top fundraising charities

7. *Welcoming Adults with Learning Difficulties at Wakefield Museums and Galleries* S Scaife in *Museums and the Education of Adults* edit Chadwick and Stannett **NIACE** (1995)

8. Binet, Alfred (1857 – 1911) French psychologist who devised a way of assessing intelligence

9. *Frames of Mind: the theory of multiple intelligences* H Gardner **Basic Books, New York** (1983)

10. *The Challenge of L'Arche* edit J Vannier **Longman and Todd, London** (1982)

11. Statistics from Introduction to *Welcoming Customers with Learning Disabilities* **Mencap** (1996)

12. *Adventures in Disability* A Tynan **Tynan Publishing** (1997)

13. *Motivation and Personality* A H Maslow **Harper & Row, New York** (1994)

14. **London Museums Service** (1991) op cit

15. *Museum Education and Disability* in *Initiatives* in *Museum Education* A Pearson edit by E Hooper-Greenhill **University of Leicester Department of Museum Studies** (1989)

16. *Something to see, something to do, somewhere to sit* J Earnescliffe *Museum Practice 4* (1997)

Initial Tasks and Constraints

The project's first task was to find out the current position on intellectual access to museums and galleries for people with learning or communication disabilities.

This was done in three ways:

- a literature search to establish the state of current published work

- contacts with people with learning disabilities, both children and adults, and those who work with them in schools, colleges, adult day centres and supported accommodation, to find out how museums are perceived by them and what they felt would make museums more successful and interesting

- visits to museums and galleries (informed by the literature search, or to see recommended displays, specialised exhibits and to experience a variety of settings)

Given the strict time limits on the project, there are many gaps in this research, particularly in the last element as opportunities to visit museums and galleries outside the central belt of Scotland were restricted. Even within that fairly small area it was not possible to visit all the places which were recommended.

Inevitably these three lines of research ran concurrently and, indeed, continued throughout the life of the project. However, for clarity, they will be dealt with separately as far as possible.

Literature Search

As there was not a great deal written specifically about access to museums and galleries for people with learning or communication disabilities, it was decided to look also at some earlier works dealing with access to the arts in general for people with a wide range of disabilities to establish the context of this research.

Early consultation of The Attenborough Report on *Arts and Disabled People* (1985)[1] *After Attenborough* (1988)[2] and *Arts for Everyone: guidance on provision for Disabled People*, Pearson (1985)[3] provided some encouraging references to learning disabilities/mental handicap, though their aim was to look at the provision for a wide range of disabilities across the full spectrum of the arts. Their main value was in their forceful message that people with disabilities must not be denied access to the arts and in stressing the value of exposure to the arts in improving the quality of life for those with disabilities.

The arts offer not only diversion and enjoyment but can provide insights into the human condition not achievable in any other way. Whether the arts are pursued primarily for their entertainment value or at a deeper level ... their importance can be even greater for people whose outlets are restricted by physical, mental or sensory impairment, than for other members of the community.[4]

The same message came through very strongly in Anne Pearson's *Arts for Everyone* which takes a very practical approach to every possible problem from the design of door furniture to the advice not to talk to the guide dog! Part 2, section 2, on *Museums, Art Galleries, Exhibition Centres and Visitor Centres* is organised, not by different disabilities, but by strategies to help, such as Mobile Exhibitions, Handling Sessions and Tape Guides. She mentions too the need for adequate lighting and clear labels which benefit all visitors and stresses the need for staff training about disability issues.

The arts offer not only diversion and enjoyment but can provide insights into the human condition not achievable in any other way.[4]

A child who has a serious difficulty with words and logical understanding may be capable of a powerful and creative aesthetic response to museum objects and have a marked ability to draw, paint or engage in another activity, such as dance or mime.

The information should be presented in such a way as to appeal not only to those members of staff who are in constant contact with the visiting public, but also to those members of the curatorial staff who are perhaps further removed from visitors and can therefore become detached and indifferent to their needs, abilities and expectations.[5]

Specifically for those with learning disabilities, Anne Pearson mentions the work done by Glasgow Museums' Education Service, by the Dorset County Museum for pupils from special schools, and the Horniman Museum Education Centre sessions for both children and adults.

The Museums and Galleries Commission's *Guidelines on Disability for Museums and Galleries in the United Kingdom* (1992 revised 1997)[6] make a number of recommendations including some which refer to people with learning disabilities. INTACT's own researches bear out the importance of many of their recommendations, particularly:

- the need for a written policy and the drawing up of an action plan on access for people with disabilities

- the requirement for all staff, including members of the governing body, to have an understanding of disability issues and have training to ensure that they understand their responsibilities in fulfilling the policy

- the need to provide alternative or supplementary means of presentation to provide access to the collections and to facilities

- the recommendation that museums should develop links with community groups to promote initiatives that would benefit people with disabilities

In *The Big Foot* Anne Pearson and Chitra Aloysius describe work done at the British Museum (where the eponymous *"foot"* was in one of the galleries), and other projects in Britain and America. The work in the British Museum was with a group of children with learning disabilities in several galleries concerned with ancient cultures, in the belief that they are entitled to the same range of educational and aesthetic experiences as their contemporaries in mainstream schools.

A child who has a serious difficulty with words and logical understanding may be capable of a powerful and creative aesthetic response to museum objects and have a marked ability to draw, paint or engage in another activity, such as dance or mime.[7]

Pearson and Aloysius report the development of the aesthetic sense and the sense of time and the growth in social empowerment in the pupils who attended the sessions. In the same book, they also refer to other British projects at the Horniman Museum, London; the Smith Art Gallery and Museum, Stirling (see too *Museums Journal*, September 1990)[8] as well as work in Dulwich, St Helens (see too *Museums Journal* March 1993)[9] Bournemouth and Sunderland. They also refer to work in America (New York, Boston and Washington). In the final chapter, they suggest the need for a wide variety of interpretive material to be used so that visitors can use more than one sensory channel to absorb information, saying finally:

As far as possible there should be greater and more imaginative use of all presentation methods which do not rely heavily on the written word.[10]

References in the works mentioned so far led to an ever-expanding list of works to consult, including articles in journals, only a few of which can be mentioned here. However, a full list is included in the bibliography and references to others are made throughout this report.

It quickly became apparent that while there was a fair amount written about provision for those with physical or sensory disabilities, there were far fewer references to those with learning or communication disabilities, and these were often mentioned incidentally. For example, accounts of touch sessions and multi-sensory displays in a museum or gallery organised for people with vision impairments might say that these were also appreciated by people with learning disabilities.[11; 12]

Some examples of work specifically related to people with learning disabilities are mentioned in *In through the front door* by Jayne Earnescliffe:

- a photography exhibition *Self-portrait* in South Wales in 1988 where people with learning disabilities were both photographers and subjects by using a cable release mechanism, and ...

- the *Sea Chest* project in Suffolk where people with learning disabilities took part in the making of the chest as well as being part of the intended audience for the finished work.

Such references to ideas or projects which could help those with learning disabilities were usually incidental. Moreover, the specific problems which this group have in understanding information which is not clearly presented were not generally recognised, nor was the need for a multi-sensory approach to give alternative means of access. In a similar way, information about 'hands-on', experiential or interactive displays is often relegated to chapters about children in museums as if adults do not enjoy the chance to try these too.

However some useful ideas came from current theories about how people, particularly adults, learn. Several contributors to both *Museums and the Education of Adults*[13] and *Developing Museum Exhibitions for Lifelong Learning*[14] refer to these theories. Equally, research on the way museum visitors behave and interact with displays, which recognises that most people come to a museum for a social and recreational experience rather than a purely educational one, is very relevant to access for people with learning disabilities. This is an area which will be discussed further.

Some American and European Perspectives

The earliest references found specifically to people with learning disabilities and museums were from America, in a series of booklets published by the Metropolitan Museum of Art, New York.[15; 16; 17] In spite of the outdated terminology and the rather didactic approach, concentrating on the educational aspects of the programmes, these give sensible advice on practical matters and show a real desire to make museums more open to this group of people.

They refer to problems which are still with us today unfortunately; such as that some museum staff feel that their institution is a place for people of superior intelligence only or are excessively concerned about possible security hazards.

The attitude of Charles K Steiner, then Project Director at the Metropolitan Museum of Art, is very enlightened for the time, despite the outdated terminology. He explains in the Introduction to '*Museum Education for Retarded Adults*' that:

As far as possible there should be greater and more imaginative use of all presentation methods which do not rely heavily on the written word.[10]

Museums and galleries which are respected institutions and are seen as highly valued community resources can send out influential signals to the general public if they are seen to be making an effort to include people who are often regarded as of little account.

... museums should be a resource for the broadest range of people. Because they cannot speak out for themselves, the mentally retarded (sic) have been traditionally neglected by museums.[18]

This admirable desire to open up museum collections to a wider public resulted largely from the passing of the USA's 1973 Rehabilitation Act, in particular to section 504 which prohibits discrimination by any institution in receipt of Federal funding.

Steiner recognises that some members of the general public might react adversely to programmes for people with learning disabilities taking place in the public galleries of the museum. In his paper *Museum Programs for the Mentally Disabled*[19] he suggests the best way of dealing with this is to demonstrate the museum's commitment to people with disabilities.

This can be done by displaying prominently the information about programmes for them and making sure that promotional material for travelling exhibitions is in an accessible format and includes information such as the location of accessible rest-rooms (toilets). Brochures advertising art programmes for people with disabilities should have an example of a work of art on the cover, not a picture of someone with a disability.

This is an important message which cannot be overstressed. The peculiar stigma of being labelled as having a learning disability has already been mentioned. Museums and galleries which are respected institutions and are seen as highly valued community resources can send out influential signals to the general public if they are seen to be making an effort to include people who are often regarded as of little account.

While inclusion was the ideal, in fact many of the early initiatives for improving access for people with learning disabilities took the form of special programmes of tours or workshops rather than trying to make the whole museum more accessible – which is rather more difficult.

One obstacle to inclusion is the negative attitude to people with a learning disability both by the non-disabled public as identified by Steiner earlier, and by some museum staff who have no experience of meeting learning-disabled individuals.

A book which sought to address this issue for tour guides and docents (American term for volunteer guides, usually students) is Jan Majewski's *Part of your general public is disabled*, Smithsonian Institution (1987).[20] As the title suggests, she is including people with a wide range of disabilities as part of the general public rather than a group which is set apart. She states in the Introduction that her guidelines are to make disabled people welcome members of *regular* tour groups and offers ideas for adapting tours so that the museum or historic site becomes more accessible to *everyone* (both italics hers).

There are chapters on people with Mental Retardation, Learning Disabilities (which she uses for dyslexia, perceptual problems etc), and Communication Disabilities. They contain much sensible practical advice which is still highly relevant, despite the now dated terminology. She recommends that guides should encourage participation by presenting multi-sensory tours where people are doing things together and individuals are not singled out, asking open-ended questions, selecting objects which visitors can relate to their own experience and looking for a main concrete theme which ties the tour together.

Published after the Americans with Disabilities Act of 1990, *The Accessible Museum* has a Preface by Dianne Pilgrim, a museum director with a physical disability, saying:

Our museums of art, design, science and history should be accessible to everyone. The truth is that what is being done in the name of access for persons with disabilities will make everyone's daily life easier ... Some of the most impressive programs in this book are the ones that are inclusive. Rather than devising projects for people with special needs (ie older people, visually impaired individuals etc), educational programs should speak to multiple voices, concerns, needs and interests.[21]

The book itself describes programmes to improve access across a range of disabilities at a zoo, an aquarium and an historic building, as well as at a number of museums and galleries with widely differing collections. It refers to the extensive on-going programmes for people with disabilities at the Metropolitan Museum of Art, New York, and also has a comprehensive bibliography.

In her account of the *New England Lifezones* exhibit at the Boston Museum of Science, Betty Davidson, the exhibit planner, is quoted as saying:

You are reaching everybody by providing different modalities of learning. They can experience it by smelling, feeling, listening: they don't have to read if they don't want to or can't. The multi-sensory approach is a very valuable one. It doesn't need to be elaborate, but it's important to give people choices of how they access information ... The important thing is to make people welcome and to give them a meaningful experience.[22]

In *Museums without Barriers*, ICOM (1992), there are accounts of courses and workshops specifically for adults and children with learning disabilities in Germany and Poland.[23; 24] There is also a paper by Louis Aven, about the setting up of the Cité des Sciences et de l'Industrie at La Villette, Paris, where he praises the study of an exhibit about the steel industry by a group of young *"mentally handicapped"* people who had fully grasped the essential approach.[25]

Our museums of art, design, science and history should be accessible to everyone.

Adult Learning in Museums

Though the main focus of INTACT's research has been on the provision for adults with learning or communication disabilities, some writers on adult education in general set off a number of lines of enquiry. Eilean Hooper-Greenhill's *A Museum Educator's Perspective* suggests that museums and galleries provide very suitable opportunities for lifelong learning to take place, though she says:

we are still not maximising the museum as a place of relevance and interest to all.[26]

She also mentions the need to become more concerned with the quality of visitor experience, the need to evaluate the provision and ...

... to develop an understanding across the museum of the learning needs of adults. Such needs range across different forms of intelligence and different learning styles.

This paper, along with other writings of Eilean Hooper-Greenhill, and those of Howard Gardner on multiple intelligences, led to further reading about the variety of learning methods and how adult learning differs from that of children. This will be dealt with in the section on learning in museums.

Guidelines on Access and Exhibition Design

There are a number of publications which deal with these matters, for example the MGC's *Guidelines on Disability for Museums and Galleries in the United Kingdom*[27] MGC's *Disability Resource Directory*[28] and *Des Visites Confortables pour Tous* (1992)[29] obtainable from the Cité des Sciences et de l'Industrie at la Villette, Paris.

Also relevant in this area, though not specifically about museums and galleries, are James Holmes-Siedle's *Barrier-free Design*[30] (1996) and the English Tourist Board's *Tourism for All: providing accessible visitor attractions* (1994).[31]

Even more recent are the Smithsonian Institution's *Guidelines for Accessible Exhibition Design* (1996)[32] Gail Nolan's *Designing Exhibitions to include People with Disabilities*[33] NMS (1997), and the draft Metropolitan Museum of Art's *Standards Manual for Signs and Labels*[34] (1995). The first two of these include references to people with learning disabilities.

Unfortunately, while all of these publications include very important points about many aspects of disability access, no single one covers all areas. It should be noted too that some of the diagrams in these publications referring to the possible reaching distance of wheelchair users are rather optimistic. Many wheelchair users with cerebral palsy have limited upper body movement and strength so such statistics must be taken as the maximum reach. Where wheelchair users have no knee or even toe space to get close to a display, there should be larger print on any labels.

It is not always recognised that wheelchair users, and others with mobility problems who prefer to use lifts, may have to cover more ground than the able bodied if they arrive at a different point from the designed entrance to a display. As this difficulty can arise on several floors of a large building, the extra distance may be considerable. It is also intolerable to expect wheelchair users to spend more than a very short time looking sideways at displays as they move along (see the reference above to limited upper body movement). This can sometimes arise because there is not enough space for people to keep turning to look straight on at the displays, but it must not be regarded as an adequate alternative to proper provision.

In many of these there are a number of suggestions for helping those with sight impairment which would also help people with learning disabilities. *Tourism for All* gives some helpful details about accessible wayfinding information, and the Metropolitan Museum's Standards are also useful, giving very detailed guidelines about print sizes on signs and labels. But, being American, all measurements are in inches.

There is no one set of guidelines which gives all the answers and, to cover the needs of people with learning disabilities, it is necessary to consult a number of works. Because of this, there is no substitute for consulting people with learning and other disabilities themselves for advice about improving access to a particular collection and building.

This brief summary of some of the main sources which were consulted is given to illustrate the background to the subsequent research. These sources also influenced the evolution of ideas for the pilot projects.

Learning Disabilities Contacts

INTACT already had a number of contacts which were useful as a starting point for this part of the research. However, initially all the adult day centres and further education colleges with special needs departments in the Edinburgh area were approached.

The Education section of the National Museums of Scotland already had contacts with a number of special schools through its programme of regular handling training courses for teachers, so we did not approach all the local special schools at the beginning of the project. However, through links with teachers who were already using the handling materials, contacts were made with a number of special schools. The reasons for focusing the main attention of the project on provision for adults have already been explained.

It was important to talk directly with students and members of day centres to get their views at first hand, rather than just talking to members of staff. A number of visits were made in the first few months of the project to such places, and views were obtained personally from members of students' or users' councils, and in Glasgow from the Key Housing Tenants' Group. Members of the local People First group, an advocacy organisation for people with learning disabilities, also gave their opinions.

So this research was based on the current perceptions about museums and galleries by people with learning disabilities and those who work with them and care for them. While most of the comments were given in the course of discussions, one written example came from trainees at the SHIRLIE Project (a training centre in Inverness for adults with learning disabilities, whose initials stand for Support, Help, Initiative, Recreation, Leisure, Independence and Education).

1. The writing in the museum is clear, though too small for some of our trainees.

2. Some of the writing, for instance on Geology, has words that most of us find difficult to understand.

3. There was a lot to see and learn even for those who can't read. The stuffed animals, videos and model people made it more interesting. The fact that you could touch the animals helped.

4. Staff are very helpful. They take time answering questions and never made you feel that they were eager to get rid of you. This again is helpful for those who can't read or don't understand everything but you would have to take the initiative.

5. It would be helpful if there were more activities that can be used to explain matters.

From the various contacts, we were able to draw on a pool of people in the Edinburgh area concerned with learning disabilities, mainly members of staff, but not exclusively so, who could bring groups of students or centre users to look at particular displays, try out something such as an audio guide, come to workshops and so on. Their input in terms of ideas was invaluable, as was the feedback on such visits. Like staff in museums, people who work in day centres and college special needs departments are exceedingly busy, and INTACT is very grateful for the time they spared to make suggestions and give encouragement and feedback.

The results of these consultations agreed with the findings of other exercises, apart from one element. This was the very strong feeling which came from the extremely small

Staff are very helpful. They take time answering questions and never made you feel that they were eager to get rid of you.

... staff training in disability awareness and the recognition of the fact that everyone has the right to enjoy museum and gallery displays is absolutely vital.

number of people with learning disabilities who felt that they had been directly discriminated against. The problems were mainly with a tiny proportion of museum attendants or front of house staff whom these people felt had treated them badly because of their disabilities.

While it must be stressed that this happened in only a very few instances and to a very small proportion of the people we consulted, it is an extremely serious issue which must be addressed if we are to have any success in encouraging people with learning and communication disabilities to visit museums and galleries.

It takes only one such incident, when a person with a learning disability is made to feel unwelcome, to undo a great deal of good work and to dissuade the person concerned, along with his/her family or friends, from ever setting foot in a museum or gallery again. The resulting undermining of that person's confidence and the belittling of someone already vulnerable are quite inexcusable. For this reason, staff training in disability awareness and the recognition of the fact that everyone has the right to enjoy museum and gallery displays is absolutely vital.

Museum Visits and Contacts

We are most grateful to the many staff in museums and galleries across the UK who expressed interest and support and gave up time from busy schedules to talk, explain what they were doing and make suggestions for other possible contacts.

Early visits included museums, galleries, historic buildings and some 'visitor centres', large and small, national and local, old and new. Many of these visits, for example to the British Museum, the Horniman, Wakefield Museums and Art Galleries, the Cité des Sciences et de l'Industrie in Paris and Glasgow Museums and Art Galleries, were prompted by references in the literature.

Sometimes there was a contact with a curator and it was possible to learn directly what that establishment was trying to do and what problems it faced; in other places visits were anonymous and the accessibility of the displays was assessed from personal experience of being with people with learning disabilities.

It is impossible to detail these visits, but certain themes have emerged. There follow a few examples from each theme of the variety of excellent work being done, as well as brief reference to some examples of displays which were less accessible for whatever reasons.

Within some of the larger institutions there was often a great variation: some displays were new or had been refurbished, while others were in need of modernisation. In a large institution with on-going programmes of temporary exhibitions as well as of updating permanent galleries, this seems inevitable given the stringent limits on money and staff time.

Provision for people with learning disabilities

Work done specifically for this group included the Intellectual Access Audit carried out at the Hancock Museum in Newcastle.[35] The Access Auditors were from Skills for People and from a local special school and they commended the variety of 'hands-on' materials, which also impressed INTACT. The auditors recommended clearer instructions for interactives, clearer signage and a plea for more information in audio form. These are issues which the museum has already started to address.

Anne Tynan's *See Me* was an exhibition *"for and about people with special needs"* which ran at the Science Museum, London, from January to June 1996. Both the exhibition content and the display methods aimed to appeal to a wide group of people. Information was provided in large print, Braille and Makaton (a sign language used by many people with learning disabilities). It was designed to awaken awareness and to encourage visitors to reflect upon issues related to disability. A number of workshops took place, some attended by groups of people with learning disabilities from local colleges or centres.

The guide for people with learning disabilities, *A Touch of Bucks*, which was produced by the Buckinghamshire County Museum at Aylesbury, will be referred to in detail in the section on Interpretation.

Accessible displays

Buckinghamshire County Museum provided also an excellent example of a modular lay-out with a very impressive combination of object-based displays arranged in themes such as "Wood and Woodland", "Clay Country" and "Lacemaking", along with plenty of 'hands-on' material including a mammoth's tooth, audio-visual touch screens, easy to understand labels and large print flip-books. For those who want still more information, the InfoRoom has a collections database, along with books and digitised copies of the museum's photographic collection.[36]

Motherwell Heritage Centre has a lively multimedia approach, backed up by a local history database which visitors can consult. The centre gives information at various levels to satisfy a range from the casual visitor to someone with a specialist interest.

Another example of the main messages being readily accessible to people with learning disabilities and non-academic members of the public is the Fish Gallery in the Royal Museum of Scotland, Edinburgh. This has been described in a Museums Journal article, *Underwater overview.*[37] Ingenious lighting gives visitors the impression that they are entering an underwater ambience where fish, large and small, singly or in shoals, are suspended in their cases. The effect is highly dramatic and displays such as the sharks and the sunfish have maximum impact.

The information is organised in a recognis-able hierarchy and some of it, for example where particular species come from, is given non-verbally. There are sound effects, a video on how fish move and labels which pose questions such as *"What is a fish?"* and let you think about this before giving the answer under a flap. The "how fish eat" display is illustrated by implements such as a sieve and nutcrackers and there is a touchscreen computer terminal on 'Sharkfax'. While some of these elements work better than others, this is a very creditable attempt to get across some quite complex messages.

Welcoming publicity

Among other initiatives, Wakefield Museums and Galleries specifically welcomed people with disabilities on their *Exhibitions and Events* leaflets.

People with disabilities.
We welcome disabled people and are keen to make your visit an enjoyable one. We can't make big changes, but we're making small ones. Pick up our new Building Information Sheets for details of our facilities ... and problems! If we cause you difficulties don't turn away – please get in touch.

Also mentioned in these leaflets, under Educational and Community Outreach, are

> 'hands-on' workshops and talks on all sorts of topics using real museum objects and art works

for schools and community groups.

Science-based education

A museum in France which was specifically designed to be accessible to all visitors is the Cité des Sciences et de l'Industrie at La Villette, Paris. This was a revelation in terms of the educational provision at all levels of age and ability, the commitment to access for people with physical, sensory or learning disabilities, and the number and variety of interactive displays, including those which were computer-based. Tours and workshops are organised for people with particular disabilities, and there is an impressive variety of interactive displays to make aspects of science comprehensible and interesting for everyone.

> Images, sounds and written texts complement each other, offering a multiple approach to knowledge ... To understand an ever-changing universe, you can touch, handle and play, constantly making discoveries and asking questions. (Introduction to the *Miniguide*, English Version, first edition).

Among the many examples of this philosophy: within the "Space" area, there were opportunities to launch a water-powered rocket and visit a simulated orbital station to experience something of the living and working conditions of astronauts; and in "Images", one could focus images on a screen in the giant darkroom as if inside a camera, or try out some of the special lighting effects to vary the atmosphere of a film shot.

Though the Cité is, strictly, a Science Centre rather than a museum, it is an impressive example of what can be done if there is money available for both education and access. The signage, which used many easily-identified icons, made it easy to find where displays and facilities were, and the labels and instructions (in English, German, Italian and Spanish as well as French) were clear and easy to read.

On a completely different scale is Satrosphere in Aberdeen, a hands-on science discovery centre with a welcoming atmosphere. This is an excellent demonstration of what can be done with a lot of ingenuity and dedication in a small space with limited resources.

Other displays of interest were "Creepy Crawlies" at the Natural History Museum, and the Materials Gallery at the Science Museum, both in London.

'Hands-on' interactives

There are a great many illustrations of interesting interactive displays, some as simple as lift up labels, large jigsaws (sometimes magnetic), or net-making. Interesting examples were found at Verdant Works, Dundee (rope-making and weavers' sign language), *St Kilda Explored*, a temporary exhibition at Kelvingrove Art Gallery and Museum, Glasgow (including an archaeological "dig") and in the Discovery Museum, Newcastle, where *A Soldier's Life*[38] featured peepholes for younger children, a 'square-bashing' exercise in front of a mirror and a board game.

Another excellent resource is the Open Museum, part of the City of Glasgow's Museums and Galleries. This has a number of ready-made items, such as the popular "Olive, the Dinner Lady" model, and handling kits which can be borrowed by community groups. Alternatively the staff will help a local group set up their own display, for example to mark a centenary.

Computer interactives

Imaginative uses of computers could be seen at several places. Croydon Clocktower's touch-screen computers in 'Lifetimes' were very easy to use and, in conjunction with the actual objects, gave a lot of interesting information about Croydon's past and the people who lived there in an accessible form with pictures and audio. This was a good example of computer-based information enhancing the displays, rather than being detached from them. Other interesting computer programmes were at Verdant Works in Dundee where visitors can compare the lives of rich and poor families, at the Horniman Museum, Forest Hill, London and at the micro-gallery in the National Gallery, London where visitors can pursue themes like "Portraits" and "Still Life" and devise and print out their own individual tour of the gallery.

Live interpreters and facilitators

Examples of these include setpiece short plays, such as those at the Royal Armouries, Leeds; costumed guides animating an area like the "Victorian Kitchen" at Callendar House, Falkirk; and in houses, shops and on the streets of museums like Beamish and the Black Country Museum.

The National Museums of Scotland ran a programme of sessions by 'Dr What?' who introduced a selection of objects from a 'Time Machine' module during the school holidays in the summer of 1997 in the Royal Museum, Edinburgh. Costumed interpreters were available at times during the temporary *Over the Threshold* exhibition about the Scottish Home and their "Discovery Room" has various 'hands-on' elements to be explored along with computer interactives and is staffed by facilitators. This has run over a number of years, has had several 'themes', and has toured to various venues in Scotland.

Art Galleries

Art Galleries which have done work to improve access for people with a variety of disabilities include the Laing in Newcastle where *Art on Tyneside*[39] has a 'hands-on' approach, sets the works in an historical context and tries to encourage a wide audience to visit, and the City Art Centre in Edinburgh which puts on a variety of popular and often innovative, temporary exhibitions such as the multi-sensory *Changing Perceptions*. Glasgow's new Gallery of Modern Art has an interactive area in the basement which includes a fibre-optic tunnel (big enough for a wheelchair user) which responds by flashing and changing colour as someone passes through it.

The places mentioned are only a small sample of the displays seen. We are well aware that there is a great deal of work going on in other institutions. Some we know about but have been unable to credit here, but there may be others of which we are totally ignorant.

There are also a few less good displays which are worth mentioning as examples of some of the problems which face people with learning disabilities. In these cases we have preserved anonymity.

The negative side

Too many museums, new as well as old, still display objects behind glass and poorly lit, without any context to make them meaningful, difficult to see for wheelchair users, and with far too much reliance on written text to provide information.

Some have taken on board modern technology and seem to think that a few computers are the answer to bringing displays up to date, with very little consideration as to the relevance of the programmes. Others have been seduced by designers into producing displays which look wonderful, but convey little information to the non-specialist, or have labels in unusual shapes or colours which are unreadable because of poor contrast, poor lighting and/or too small print. Many museums and galleries are still presenting most of their information in written format, too often in large indigestible chunks.

Sometimes the best of intentions can be frustrated. An example of this was an audio guide in simple English for people with learning disabilities at an historic site. Unfortunately, this had not been updated to take account of changes in the displays (as the ordinary audio guide had been) so that the rearrangement made a nonsense of instructions like *"Now turn to your left and look for..."*

Other examples come from modern displays where the problems are the result of lack of thought and consultation. A number of problems arose in the use of computers. One small museum took technology to the extreme and had computers equipped with video-discs and sound throughout. This meant that it was possible for visitors to set off three or four of these at once in a small area, so that none could be heard properly. Another had a range of computers in a small area, each one equipped with a carefully designed mouse, placed on the right of the screen, fitting the right hand and fingers of the visitor very comfortably, but extremely hard to use for anyone who was left-handed.

There were several instances of computers set into solid plinths, or even into the vertical side of a display, giving wheelchair users no knee or footplate room to get close enough to use the device.

Disappointingly, a new and quite expensive visitor centre offered an audio-visual interactive experience which turned out not to be available to wheelchair users because of stairs, a very narrow walkway and the fire risk. The audio commentary was given over various sound effects (including cannon fire) and used difficult and often antiquated vocabulary and sentence constructions, presumably in the belief that this would give authenticity. While there were some real objects displayed behind glass in a waiting area and the visitor centre itself was situated in an area with which it had an historic connection, most of the 'experience' was completely contrived with model figures in a reconstructed setting with replica tools, utensils and weapons.

A number of approaches were made to museums or galleries around Britain through names suggested by existing contacts or as the result of a reference in a book or journal. Some of these were extremely useful and helpful while a few came to nothing, through no fault of anyone concerned, perhaps because the approach was made at the wrong time or the person who might have been interested had moved on. Useful contacts were made in France, the United States and Canada. These included Lon Dobinsky of Ontario, Canada, co-ordinator of the *Reading in the Museum* Project.[40] which he wrote about in *Museums and Literacy: a natural partnership*, JEM 18.

References

1. *Arts and Disabled people: The Attenborough Report* **Carnegie UK Trust** (1985)

2. *After Attenborough* **Carnegie UK Trust** (1988)

3. *Arts for Everyone* A Pearson **Carnegie UK Trust** (1985) p25

4. Carnegie (1985) op cit

5. Pearson (1985) op cit

6. *Guidelines on Disability for Museums and Galleries in the United Kingdom* **Museums and Galleries Commission** (1992) updated as *Access to Museums and Galleries for People with Disabilities* (1997)

7. *Museums and Children with Learning Difficulties – The Big Foot* Pearson and Aloysius **British Museum Press** (1994)

8. *Smith goes Green* R Nicholson *Museums Journal* (September 1990)

9. *Open House, Open Mind* K Moore *Museums Journal* (March 1993)

10. Pearson and Aloysius (1994) op cit

11. *In through the front door* J Earnescliffe **The Arts Council of Great Britain** (1992)

12. *Touch exhibitions in the United Kingdom* A Pearson in *Museums without Barriers* **ICOM** (1985)

13. *Museums and the Education of Adults* edit Chadwick and Stannett **NIACE** (1995)

14. *Developing Museum Exhibitions for Lifelong Learning* edit G Durbin **GEM/Stationery Office** (1996)

15. *Museum Education for Retarded Adults: reaching out to a neglected audience* C K Steiner **Metropolitan Museum of Art, New York** (1979)

16. *Museums and the Disabled* C K Steiner **Metropolitan Museum of Art, New York** (1979)

17. *Help for the Special Educator* C K Steiner **Metropolitan Museum of Art, New York** (1981)

18. Steiner (1979) op cit

19. *Museum Programs for the Mentally Disabled* C K Steiner in *Museums without Barriers* **ICOM** (1991)

20. *Part of your general public is disabled* J Majewski **Smithsonian Institution, Washington** (1987)

21. *The Accessible Museum: Model Programs of Accessibility for Disabled and Older People* **AAM** (1992) *Preface*

22. **AAM** (1992) op cit Chapter on *The Museum of Science, Boston*

23. *The National Museum of Fine Art in Karlsruhe, Germany* G Reising in *Museums without Barriers* **ICOM** (1991)

24. *Services for the Mentally handicapped at the Royal Castle, Warsaw* J D Artymowski in *Museums without Barriers* **ICOM** (1991)

25. *The work of the Commission on the Disabled at the Cité des Sciences et de l'Industrie, Paris, and the Charter for the Disabled* L Aven in *Museums without Barriers* **ICOM** (1991)

26. *A Museum Educator's Perspective* E Hooper-Greenhill in *Museums and the Education of Adults* edit Chadwick & Stannett **NIACE** (1995)

27. Guidelines on *Disability for Museums and Galleries in the United Kingdom* **Museums and Galleries Commission** (1992) updated as *Access to Museums and Galleries for People with Disabilities* (1997)

28. *Disability Resource Directory for Museums* **Museums and Galleries Commission** (1993, Supplement 1997)

29. *Des Visites Confortable pour Tous* (1992) obtainable from the Cité des Sciences et de l'Industrie at la Villette, Paris.

30. *Barrier-free Design* J Holmes-Siedle **Butterworth Architecture** (1996)

31. *Tourism for All: providing accessible visitor attractions* **English Tourist Board** (1994)

32. *Guidelines for Accessible Exhibition Design* **Smithsonian Institution, Washington** (1996)

33. *Designing Exhibitions to include People with Disabilities* G Nolan **NMS** (1997)

34. *Standards Manual for Signs and Labels* (1995 draft) **Metropolitan Museum of Art, New York**

35. *Disability Resource Directory for Museums* **Museums and Galleries Commission** (1997 Supplement, Section 16)

36. *A Touch of Bucks* in *Museum Practice* issue 5 (1997)

37. *Underwater overview* P Davis *Museums Journal* (February 1998)

38. *A Soldier's Life* in *Museum Practice* issue 5 (1997)

39. *Art on Tyneside* in *Museums Journal* (Feb 1992)

40. *Museums and Literacy: a natural partnership* L Dobinsky Co-ordinator of the *Reading in the Museum* Project, *Journal of Education in Museums 18* (1997)

Museums are the outcome of human curiosity, of the desire to learn. It is hard to imagine anyone visiting a museum for more than a few minutes without learning something new, whatever their age or formal educational background. Museums are resources for all kinds of learning and because their stock-in-trade is composed of objects, which can be seen and sometimes handled, they can have a greater immediacy of impact than most other learning resources if used imaginatively. Professor Lalage Bown, Foreword to *Object Lessons – The Role of Museums in Education* edit Sue Mitchell HMSO (1997).

People visit museums for a variety of reasons: to study, for recreation, as a social activity, to see something unusual or unique, or to look at a specific exhibition that interests them. These diverse motives apply also to people with learning disabilities, whether they come independently, in a family party or with a group from a day centre or college.

Education in a Museum Context

Along with the care and collection of objects or works of art, a museum or gallery has a duty to allow public access and so provide educational opportunities, whether formal or informal. However some museums see this 'educational' role as solely the function of the Education Department and not something necessarily permeating all their activities, while others (the majority of museums taking part in the first questionnaire survey undertaken for David Anderson's *A Common Wealth*) had no member of staff with specific responsibility for education. Anderson says:

even in those museums that employ educational specialists, only 22% invite these staff to contribute actively to the gallery design process[1]

and argues that this is a serious concern.

Educational provision may cover a wide area including school visits and workshops, guided tours for members of the public or special interest groups, talks by curators, evening lectures, study sessions, and outreach activities. Even where these are not provided solely by members of education staff, education is often seen as something which the museum dispenses and the visitor absorbs.

In *Beyond museums: objects and culture*,[2] Anderson proposes that more time and resources in existing museums should be given to self-directed learning and suggests that:

It is strange that we have persisted in using curriculum-driven education as our predominant methodology in museums, when the great majority of our visitors learn informally. In the museum context, programmed learning floats like a ship on a sea of self-directed learning.

Museum designers and curators often go to considerable lengths to direct the learning of their visitors. They create displays which are often quite strictly laid out to convey a particular message or theme and the information presented, from introductory panels to the details given along the pre-planned route through the display, are all designed to reinforce this. Displays are cunningly designed to lead visitors along the pre-determined route and to discourage them from exiting before the end.

This type of display technique is undoubtedly intended to be instructive but, like the tours, lectures and talks referred to above, it is a one-way process with little reference to the priorities of the visitor.

Museums are resources for all kinds of learning and because their stock-in-trade is composed of objects, which can be seen and sometimes handled, they can have a greater immediacy of impact than most other learning resources if used imaginatively.
Professor Lalage Bown

This would imply that museum exhibitions should cater for the different learning profiles of visitors by providing a multi-sensory experience so that they have the chance to participate in their own learning.

Such displays tend to be focused on a predominantly older, white, middle-class audience who are more used to having information presented to them in an organised academic way. They are geared towards people with high verbal ability who will often have some prior knowledge of the content.

However, this is not how most people learn, especially not in an informal context, which is how they would regard a museum visit. Even this older, white, middle-class audience is not homogeneous and they too will leave a rigidly structured exhibition if it does not meet their needs.

Howard Gardner in *Frames of Mind*, referred to in a previous section, suggests that people have different learning styles, which are parallel, not hierarchical, though our society tends to give more importance to the linguistic and logical/ mathematical categories than others such as spatial, bodily-kinaesthetic, musical and inter-personal.

This would imply that museum exhibitions should cater for the different learning profiles of visitors by providing a multi-sensory experience so that they have the chance to participate in their own learning. Some visitors will prefer mostly text-based information such as labels, information panels and exhibition guidebooks; some will enjoy information presented through interactive computers or by audio guides; while others will welcome the chance to touch. Depending on the learning context, the same visitor may wish to use several different modes. As Richard Wood says:

> The chance to press a button or make something happen confers a sense of well-being, of being in control. Museums can be great intimidators.[3]

Much can be learnt about an object by being able to handle it, even if it is not fine enough to be in a display case. For example, without allowing visitors to touch different types of animal fur, it is difficult to

Handling Session

explain how they are adapted to the needs of the animals, such as waterproofing or providing warmth in an extreme climate. Also the inevitable wear which will occur on a 'touchable' specimen explains without words why the best specimens are kept in the controlled environment of a glass case.

Elizabeth Esteve-Coll in *A Yearning for Learning* (1993) said of museums:

They encourage learning from the real – visual and material culture in all its diversity – as opposed to the simulated. They enable us to learn through our senses, especially sight and touch, as well as from the written word. [4]

Being able to handle objects is something all visitors appreciate and encourages them to remember more about what they have touched.

Handling is particularly helpful for people with learning disabilities because, as well as letting them understand aspects of the objects they might not grasp if the information is given verbally, it also encourages social interaction, discussion and concentration. This was demonstrated by the groups who attended sessions at the Royal Museum, Edinburgh described in the pilot project section.

The learning which takes place in museums does not consist solely of the acquisition of facts. It should include a whole range of experiences from the 'wow' factor, through an understanding of change and development over time, to aesthetic appreciation. As Lisa Roberts points out:

Learning in museums includes emotional, social, contemplative, recreational and attitudinal aspects, all of which have been documented by researchers seeking to characterise the nature of the visitor experience. An understanding of these aspects is essential to developing exhibits that reach learners in ways meaningful to them. [5]

She also maintains that museum educators are the link between the content of an exhibition and the audience. They have to represent the interests of the wide variety of visitors who come to see the displays and to help to achieve the necessary balance between the collection of objects and its curatorial/ conservation requirements and the interpretation of the collection.

The Visitors' Perspective

The majority of adult visitors will not come in contact with the organised educational activities provided by the museum. Their learning will tend to be casual and random depending on what displays they elect to look at; they will pick and choose, browse or cruise past displays until something catches their eye. Visitor behaviour in museums has been likened to that of casual shoppers in a department store by Falk in *The use of time as a measure of visitor behaviour and exhibit effectiveness*. [6]

Adult visitors come with their own agenda and want to be able to absorb any learning from museum displays into their own experience. Their participation in the learning process is voluntary and they can ignore what does not interest them or even leave. Museums have to recognise that learning is a two-way process for adults and they must be prepared to enter into a dialogue so that it becomes an active process for visitors. As Elaine Heumann Gurian says:

Exhibitions are places of free choice. Try as we might, the public continually thwarts our attempts to teach incrementally in an

Museums have to recognise that learning is a two-way process for adults and they must be prepared to enter into a dialogue so that it becomes an active process for visitors.

Adults with learning disabilities are no different from other adults in that they prefer to learn independently. They already have their own existing knowledge, abilities and interests; what they learn in a museum must fit in with their previous experience.

> exhibition. They come when they want, leave when they want and look at what they want while they are there. Therefore linear installations often feel like forced marches.[7]

Often the most meaningful learning takes place when visitors see something, perhaps accidentally, which fits in with what they know already. Seeing a real object in a museum may provide the missing piece which links other areas of knowledge, or a tangible artefact may make sense of a previously confusing abstract idea.

> Museums are excellent environments for meaningful learning because they offer rich, multi-sensory experiences. The proper presentation of ideas through tangible objects, particularly if interactive, is a powerful device for sense-making and, thus, understanding. Falk & Dierking, *The Museum Experience*.[8]

Much learning which takes place in museums occurs in a social context. Most visitors come with a friend or in a family group. Social groups and families often point out objects in displays or read out labels to each other. In this way they share their knowledge and frequently relate what they see to other experiences which they have in common. Museum exhibits which encourage people to cluster round encourage this kind of co-operative learning.

Relevance to People with Learning Disabilities

Adults with learning disabilities are no different from other adults in that they prefer to learn independently. They already have their own existing knowledge, abilities and interests; what they learn in a museum must fit in with their previous experience. Although their disabilities may have restricted the opportunities and experience on which they base this learning, this does not mean that knowledge and understanding cannot be gained in the right context.

Like many people whose experiences of school were unhappy, adults with learning disabilities may be lacking in self-confidence. Even if they are keen to discover new areas of knowledge, they may be unsure about their ability to learn and even how to behave in a learning situation. If the museum presents them with information in a style and format that are unfamiliar and inaccessible they may feel awkward and even incapable, and it is very unlikely that they will find the visit a rewarding experience.

Professor Lalage Bown writes about museums as a resource for adult learners, mentioning the immediacy of original physical objects:

> the fact that learning is from objects means that museum collections may be used by people who do not have access to the written word, either because they have missed out on literacy altogether, or because they have a different language or a different script. Museums, in such cases, provide a possible alternative to literacy – communication through artefacts rather than writing.[9]

She also mentions the possibilities in a museum for engendering independent learning and thus empowering people.

David Jones in *The Adult Learner* (1995) points out that adults are not a homogeneous group; they have a range of educational and life experiences, and have their own value systems. He mentions *Cognitive Styles and Adult Learning* by G. Squires of Nottingham University Department of Adult Education which identifies different styles of learning, and quotes the Nottingham Androgogy (as opposed to pedagogy) Group's salient features of adult learning as:

- non-prescriptive
- continuous negotiation
- shared individual and group responsibility for learning
- valuing process as part of learning
- mutual respect[10]

These features are just as important for adults with learning disabilities as they are for any other adults.

So, because museums are object-based, rather than text-based, they are potentially areas where multi-sensory learning can take place and people with different learning styles and different intelligence profiles can learn in ways which are most appropriate to them.

Direct contact with artefacts, whether simply through sight, but better by the use of other senses as well, can develop understanding of materials, of function and design, of chronology, and of cultural differences and similarities. According to Richard Wood, original artefacts …

… are an essential raw material from which the learning experience is built.[11]

George Hein in *Evaluating a Display Adapted for People with Learning Difficulties*[12] describes the modifications made to the *New England Life Zone* display in the Boston Museum of Science. The adaptations consist of three major components plus some additional materials.

- All the dioramas received new and expanded panels with information rewritten to be easier to read and understand. Space was provided to include an audio-tape and earphone, a "smell box" and usually something to touch, such as a moose hoof

- Three dimensional presentations of some of the species in the diorama were set out so that visitors could touch them. These included two metal bird models and mounted specimens of a beaver and a bear

- Three free-standing hands-on displays related to the exhibits

The results were that 'ordinary' visitors spent more time in the gallery and more seemed to be engaged in purposeful behaviour, using different sensory modes and comparing related components of the display. The new hands-on elements attracted more visitors without decreasing the attracting power of the dioramas. When questioned about what they had learned, there was a great increase in the proportion of visitors who could name some adaptive feature which allowed an animal to live as it does.

It was found that the visitors with learning disabilities were particularly sensitive to changes in the presentation format and needed **multiple and duplicated** (ie the same information repeated in a variety of media; text, audio, graphic etc) clues to suggest how they might interact with an exhibit. George Hein draws the conclusion from this that most visitors require consistency and some repetition of information to use interactives successfully. Too often ordinary visitors find them difficult because the nature of the interaction varies and the instructions are inconsistent.

These findings are endorsed by the Smithsonian Guidelines for *Accessible Exhibition Design* which state, under "Exhibition Content":

People with cognitive disabilities may need a combination of formats. Multi-sensory presentations provide choices for the sensory channel used and interesting repetitions of key points.[13]

... help visitors to find their own way around and to make sense of what they are seeing, rather than directing the learning process along a pre-determined instructional path.

People with cognitive disabilities may need a combination of formats. Multi-sensory presentations provide choices for the sensory channel used and interesting repetitions of key points.[13]

Lest this emphasis on repetition of information be regarded as patronising, two points must be made. Firstly, many people with learning disabilities do have problems remembering things, particularly if they are unfamiliar, as a direct result of their disability. Secondly, those of us who can read and talk about historical or scientific terms like 'the Renaissance' or 'omnivorous' can very easily forget that our knowledge comes in fact from many repetitions of these terms over time and in different contexts. This gives us a wide basis for our understanding of them which has been built up gradually so that we usually cannot remember when we did not know what they meant.

People with learning disabilities, many of whom do not read, will suffer an indirect disadvantage through not having had the same opportunities to become familiar with such terms, and nor will many members of the public who have received only a basic education. Well-educated people (this includes museum designers, educators and curators) are fortunate in having this knowledge and should show patience and understanding to those who do not. They must appreciate the need to explain 'technical terms' in order to make displays accessible for those who have not had the chance to acquire this knowledge.

The Smithsonian Guidelines also suggest that, since people with learning disabilities learn best from an orderly presentation, displays should be programmed to do this.

An exhibition that reveals its topic through an obvious storyline, theme or repeated element offers landmarks, repetition and a connecting thread to follow a complex presentation.[14]

This structure, emphasised by landmarks and repetition, is very different from the rigidly organised type of displays referred to earlier. It has features which help visitors **to find their own way around** and to make sense of what they are seeing, rather than directing the learning process along a pre-determined instructional path.

An interesting comparison of a structured with a non-structured approach to a natural history exhibition can be found in John Falk's *Assessing the Impact of Exhibit Arrangement on Visitor Behaviour and Learning*.[15]

As more museums become aware, perhaps because of competition from visitor centres and theme parks, that people are no longer content to look at objects in glass cases and get all their information about them in written form, other ways of providing information are becoming more usual. These can include audio, video, graphics, objects which may be touched, guided tours, live interpretation, interactives (both lo-tech and computerised) and working exhibits. Setting objects in context such as a room setting or diorama and comparing them with present day equivalents, or, in the case of animal adaptions such as beak variations, comparing them with human tools which do a similar task, are all now common.

The variety of ways through which a museum can provide information leads naturally to the next section which deals with interpretation.

References

1. *A Common Wealth – Museums and learning in the United Kingdom* D Anderson **Department of National Heritage** (1997)

2. *Beyond museums: objects and culture* D Anderson *Journal for Education in Museums 13*, (1992)

3. *Museums Learning: a family focus* R Wood *Journal for Education in Museums 11* (1990) reprinted in *Developing Museum Exhibitions for Lifelong Learning* **GEM/Stationery Office** (1996)

4. *A Yearning for Learning* E Esteve-Coll *Museums Journal* (May 1993)

5. *Educators on Exhibition Teams: a New Role, a New Era* L C Roberts *Journal of Museum Education* (Fall 1994)

6. *The use of time as a measure of visitor behaviour and exhibit effectiveness* J Falk *Roundtable Reports 7 (4)* (1982)

7. *Noodling around with Exhibition Opportunities* E Heumann Gurian reprinted in *Developing Museum Exhibitions for Lifelong Learning* **GEM/Stationery Office** (1996)

8. *The Museum Experience* J Falk and L Dierking **Whalesback Books** (1994)

9. *An Adult Educator's Perspective* L Bown in *Museums and the Education of Adults* edit Chadwick & Stannett **NIACE** (1995)

10. *The Adult Learner* D Jones in *Museums and the Education of Adults* edit Chadwick & Stannett **NIACE** (1995)

11. *Museums, Means, and Motivation: Adult Learning in a Family Context* R Wood in *Museums and the Education of Adults* **NIACE** (1995)

12. *Evaluating a Display adapted for People with Learning Difficulties* G E Hein reprinted in *Developing Museum Exhibitions for Lifelong Learning* **GEM/Stationery Office** (1996)

13. *Accessible Exhibition Design* **Smithsonian Institution Guidelines** (1997)

14. op cit

15. *Assessing the Impact of Exhibit Arrangement on Visitor Behaviour and Learning* J Falk first published in *Curator* 36 (2) (1993) and reprinted in *Developing Museum Exhibitions for Lifelong Learning* **GEM/Stationery Office** (1996)

Where the principles of good interpretation are observed they will benefit people with learning disabilities at least as much, if not more, than they benefit the general run of visitors.

... two sides to interpretation, the message and the medium.

The Introduction to the section on Interpretation in *Museum Practice 5* says that it is:

the process of using displays and associated information to convey messages about objects and the meanings which museums attach to them; and of selecting appropriate media and techniques to communicate effectively with target audiences.[1]

Where the principles of good interpretation are observed they will benefit people with learning disabilities at least as much, if not more, than they benefit the general run of visitors. Access for all should mean that interpretation is inclusive, meaningful and relevant to the museum or gallery experience.

The early references to the subject are from the context of outdoor recreation and education, although the principles established in the 1950s in that area apply equally to indoor as to outdoor displays. The word is now increasingly used in a museum, gallery, or visitor attraction to indicate a wider purpose than education alone. It may be helpful, therefore, to restate briefly the case for, and content of, good interpretation because it should underpin all planning of displays for all visitors.

What is Interpretation?

It is not translation, and it is perhaps a pity that there is not another word for its specialised meaning in this context. According to Chambers' Dictionary, "to interpret" means "to explain the meaning of". In the context of the natural heritage, Freeman Tilden[2] defined it in 1957 as:

An educational activity which aims to reveal meanings and relationships through the use of original objects, by first-hand experience, and by illustrative media, rather than simply to communicate factual information.

As an example, he quotes how to illustrate the age of a giant sequoia tree, not by a number, but by taking a slice of it and associating its growth rings with a time line of human history, showing events which the visitor will recognise and relate to.

Tilden outlined the principles which still underlie the practice of the National Park Service in the USA and they have been re-stated in convenient and up to date form in Scottish Natural Heritage (SNH)'s *Provoke, Relate, Reveal* and in James Carter's *A Sense of Place*. They, along with the Association of Scottish Visitor Attractions (ASVA)'s, *Interpretation – a Guide*, and the papers on the subject in *Museum Practice 5*, (1997), the theme of which was Interpretation, are essential reading for anyone devising a new display.

Interpretation in museums has come about as a result of the demand from visitors to know more about the collections. They are no longer content merely to have objects identified, but want explanations, background information and ways of putting them into a context of things they already know about. James Carter says ...

... interpretation does not involve simply giving visitors fact: it aims to give them new insights, ideas, and ways of looking at or appreciating a place.[3]

The Museum Practice paper, quoted at the beginning of this section, acknowledges the two sides to interpretation, the message and the medium and a later reference to "target audiences" indicates that museums are now recognising the needs of non-academic visitors and have realised that:

objects do not speak for themselves and need the support of interpretation to make them accessible to visitors.[4]

Helen Coxall in *Issues of Museum Text*[5] points out that this message is determined by the way information is selected, which is in its turn determined by the values of the museum and the exhibition team. Both visitors and exhibition teams need to be aware of this. No exhibition can ever be wholly objective and the very act of putting something on display and providing information about it, implies value judgements.

In a gallery context, the Scottish Arts Council (SAC)'s *A Short Guide to Interpretation* states

Essentially it is about understanding communication in its many forms, about enabling exploration and creating debate, and is about the cerebral and physical engagement with art practice. It refers to the wider environment and experiences we all draw upon each moment of our lives, and can help form opinion and shape responses.[6]

Clearly the common factor in all these definitions is the communication of messages which will enable visitors to relate what they see or experience, whether in a museum, an art gallery or an outdoor area, to what they have already experienced and thus help them to enjoy and understand it more fully. Julian Spalding in *Communicating generously* warns curators against the danger of …

… erecting an unscalable barrier of knowledge around their subject.

He points out that if visitors look at an object, then at the label, then go immediately to the next object, that label has failed in its purpose:

Any form of interpretation is only valid if it makes visitors look again at the object it interprets, and with greater understanding.[7]

It is important that this communication is available for the full range of visitors. If access is to be for all, the messages must be expressed simply and directly through more than one sensory channel. However, they must be supported by serious scholarship and research. The challenge for museums and galleries is to enable visitors to obtain information about the displays in the form and at the level they prefer. Those who require it can find additional information from specialised tours, exhibition guides, workshops or access to reserve collections or databases.

It is clearly impossible to devise a presentation which will satisfy all visitors, from primary school children to serious academic researchers. However it is generally considered that a presentation which will be understood by children between 10 and 14 will satisfy many adult visitors and will greatly help people with learning disabilities.

If text is organised in a hierarchy, the casual visitor will get the main message from the first few lines, while those with a more detailed interest will be able to read further. Audio guides can be offered to help people with learning disabilities, poor literacy, visual impairment or whose first language is not English. The serious researcher can be given access to a computerised database. The National Museums of Scotland are developing MOSAICS (Museum of Scotland Advanced Interactive Computer System) as a database for objects in the Museum of Scotland, while SCRAN (Scottish Cultural Resources Access Network) is aiming to link museum and gallery databases throughout Scotland.

… enable visitors to relate what they see or experience, whether in a museum, an art gallery or an outdoor area, to what they have already experienced and thus help them to enjoy and understand it more fully.

It is worth noting that in planning the displays in the Museum of Scotland, the Trustees of the National Museums of Scotland adopted a policy that 80% of the displays should be comprehensible to at least 80% of the visitors and that 50% – messages, objects, text and information technology where appropriate – should be capable of being understood by the average 10 year old. Having geared displays to such a broad target audience, it is possible to cater for minorities by other means.

Planning Interpretation

To be successful, interpretation needs to be planned. If displays are to educate visitors and increase understanding, appreciation and awareness of their importance and relevance, they must first attract and then hold their attention. So, as SNH argue,

Effective communication is able to combine enjoyment with learning.[8]

According to Lisa Roberts in *Educators on Exhibit Teams: a New Role, a New Era*:

Interpretation is the single most basic purpose of an exhibit. Whether implicit or explicit, interpretation is embedded in the act of display – in how a thing looks, in what surrounds it, in what is said or not said about it.[9]

She points out that interpretation is the responsibility of every member of the display team: curators, designers and educators. Interpretation must, to some extent, be:

an act of negotiation – between the values and knowledge upheld by museums and those that are brought by the visitors and museum educators have a crucial role in this. According to SNH, interpretation:

- is a communication process ... It is a means to an end, not an end in itself

- reveals meanings and relationships, unlike information, which presents a series of facts

- involves wherever possible first hand experiences ... The most meaningful learning experiences come through personal contact and involvement with... the artefact.[10]

Their publication, *Provoke, Relate, Reveal* (1997), although designed primarily for environmental interpretation and based on work by Freeman Tilden, Don Aldridge and others, suggests that the aims should be to:

Provoke curiosity and interest

Relate to everyday experiences of your audience

Reveal a memorable message, and

Address **the whole story** using a unifying theme

They add that interpretation should stimulate the audience's imagination, be relevant to its needs, offer a fresh insight and be appropriate to the site or object. Presentations should be highly visual and encourage interaction.

Veverka refers to visitors retaining

10% of what they hear
30% of what they read
50% of what they see and
90% of what they do.[11]

While the percentage relating to reading is not appropriate for people with learning disabilities, there are other activities, such as studying pictures or graphics, which would have a similar recall factor.

Evaluation should always be part of the planning process. The museum will not know that the message it wishes to convey has been understood unless it finds out how visitors respond. If possible, this should be done in stages before a display is finalised. At the planning stage for the Museum of Scotland, a number of 'test bed' or prototype displays were mounted and members of the public and other invited visitors, such as people with disabilities (including learning disabled) were asked to give their opinions. For each display, a revised version was produced after some of the initial recommendations were acted upon, and further comments invited.

Many evaluation techniques are available such as visitor numbers, observation, timing how long people spend in front of displays, questionnaires, a comments book or formal interviews. However the most useful tend to be the most time consuming. There are also pitfalls. Are the visitors who spend so long in front of an exhibit fascinated by it, are they puzzling over what it means or are they discussing when they will go for tea?

Interpretive media

People learn best if a variety of media are appropriately used, appealing to as many of the senses as possible. Veverka stresses that people learn better when they are actively involved in the learning process and that what they discover for themselves generates a special and vital excitement and satisfaction. He suggests using questions to help people arrive at answers for themselves.

It may seem to be stating the obvious but different audiences require different types of interpretation, as do different subjects of display. Sometimes the nature of the exhibition or the site will determine the audience but, where institutions are anxious to enlarge the range of visitors they cater for, they may need to consider interpretation methods specifically designed to appeal to a wider public.

ASVA's useful booklet, *Interpretation – A Guide*, referred to earlier, offers seven key questions to act as prompts when planning an interpretive strategy:

Who? What? Where? Which? When? How? and Why?[12]

Media and Methods

If this wider public includes people with learning and/or other disabilities, particular ethnic groups or a family audience, interpretation methods must be varied, flexible and able to compete with other forms of mass media such as video or computer interactives. The passive experience of reading the 'book on the wall' will not satisfy visitors who want something to do and to engage with the displays.

The dilemma for museums is how to achieve this without becoming the sort of all-singing, all-dancing visitor centre, full of gadgets but with few genuine objects on display, which would alienate the visitor with a specialist interest. This is a question which can be resolved only by the institution concerned, bearing in mind its priorities.

However, judicious provision of layers of information through a variety of media afforded a solution to this dilemma for a number of establishments, including the Buckinghamshire County Museum,

People learn best if a variety of media are appropriately used, appealing to as many of the senses as possible.

Audio guides can be very helpful for people with learning disabilities and those who are not confident readers.

Aylesbury and Newcastle Discovery Museum's *A Soldier's Life*, both referred to later.

ASVA's *Interpretation – A Guide*, lists 23 possible interpretation methods from simple leaflets given to every visitor to major performance events, giving "pro"s and "con"s to assess cost, effectiveness and flexibility. This guide also emphasises the importance of deciding objectives and of evaluating the interpretive strategy for a site or a display both front-end and as an on-going exercise.

The most flexible interpretive method is the live interpreter, who may be a curator or museum educator, a volunteer guide, an attendant or custodian, an artist or craft demonstrator, a lecturer or a costumed actor. These have the ability to interact, to respond to questions and contact with them is usually a memorable experience for visitors. However they are also expensive as they have to be paid and/or trained and they can vary greatly in quality.

For people with learning disabilities this can be an ideal way of acquiring information as the live interpreter is able to tailor his/her talk to the interests of the group. However it is vital that s/he is able to relate to people with learning disabilities and is aware of possible problems. Some quite small museums who rely on volunteers, such as Abbot House, Dunfermline, have been able to offer this service very successfully where they have guides who have experience of talking and relating to this audience.

Museum warders, attendants and security guards are another potential resource to act as walking labels: discussions (at the National Museums of Scotland and elsewhere) suggest that many warders would welcome this if they were given some basic training in giving information. This would both help visitors (who like live guides) and enrich their own job satisfaction. Such a system works well at Kelvingrove Art Gallery and Museum in Glasgow, where warders are called "museum attendants" and have a much wider range of duties than security.

Anything involving electronics (audio, video or computers) tends to be costly both initially if done well, and in terms of on-going maintenance. They should be used only if there are adequate back-up facilities and staff trained to operate them and diagnose any faults. It is significant that the Cité des Sciences et de l'Industrie in Paris employs 185 technicians among their personnel. Interactive computers or video presentations which do not work are a source of irritation to the visitor and of embarrassment to the museum which houses them. The Computer Pilot Project section will give more information about using computers as a source of information in museums.

Audio guides can be very helpful for people with learning disabilities and those who are not confident readers. However, to be most useful, they should be flexible. Flexibility for visitors implies a random access system giving freedom to key in a number for the display or object they want information about and switch off when they have heard enough. For the museum or gallery, flexibility means being able to alter the information on the script.

In a gallery setting, where information is likely to relate to one work for each number to be keyed, the problem of works being moved or removed would not apply, but it could be a problem when one of several objects in a museum display case is moved. Some audio guide systems already in use can give the museum or gallery feedback on what pictures or objects the visitor sought information. They can even note if s/he got bored and cut the commentary off before it was finished.

A very new development, still at the experimental stage, is the 'intelligent label explorer', Ilex. The Ilex project is being jointly undertaken by the National Museums of Scotland and the Human Communication Resource Centre at the Department of Artificial Intelligence at Edinburgh University. The idea is that Ilex will not only take account of visitors' own interests, remembering the exhibits already called up, but will also take opportunities to tell them about underlying themes and objectives in an exhibition. This is likely to be in the form of earphones attached to a handset, which each visitor will be able to programme with a personal profile – interests, education level, how long s/he intends to stay – before setting off to tour an exhibition. The visitor then points the handset at a sensor mounted under the object s/he wants to know about and this will communicate with a central computer which transmits the information back to the visitor's machine.

While it will be some time before the problems of machine-generated text are overcome, and still longer before such a system is widely available, Ilex has considerable potential for tailoring the information which visitors receive about museum objects to individual interests and learning styles. If a smart card can tell the supermarket the sort of food or soap powder you buy and target their marketing accordingly, a machine that can learn your interests in a museum by noting what objects you want to know about is scarcely far fetched.

Tape tours, often recorded by museum staff themselves, are flexible from the institution's point of view, but less so for the user who is 'locked in', and the sound quality tends not to be good. However, with the possibilities of solid state recording devices and DAT tape, the quality may soon improve and changing the message may become easier.

INTACT obtained two 'talking labels' (one purchased and one loaned) and these were trialled at museums in Dundee and Inverness. One, with an earpiece for individual listening, was used in Inverness as part of their railway display and the other, with a speaker which could be heard in the immediate area, was used in Dundee to provide information about Professor D'Arcy Thomson, a nineteenth century collector. Both types were used and enjoyed by a variety of visitors and museum staff found them easy to record on and appreciated the ability to change the message whenever they wanted.

The previous section on *Learning in Museums* referred to the New England Life Zone which used a multi-sensory approach including 'hands-on' experiences, or relating objects to things that are familiar, as well as to some reasons why the use of different sensory channels is particularly relevant for people with learning disabilities. However it is possible to go too far in this, as it may be preferable to increase access by adding multi-sensory interactive components to traditional display cases rather than by eliminating the cases altogether. Some interactive displays are rather thin on actual objects and so lose the impact of the original collection.

Text in the form of labels and information panels is the most traditional method of interpretation. But it is not cheap to produce if it is to be accurate, well written, well presented and in a durable format. Questions of readability will be covered in the next section.

Written guides to a particular exhibition or area have some of the same disadvantages

Text in the form of labels and information panels ... is not cheap to produce if it is to be accurate, well written, well presented and in a durable format.

as other written forms of information. They may include illustrations which can be helpful to less confident readers and the fact that they are portable and can therefore be read while seated is a benefit. Provided they are free or the cost is low, they are appreciated by visitors as a reminder of what they have seen.

A special Case Study

A Touch of Bucks[13] a guide for people with learning disabilities, was produced by the Buckinghamshire County Museum in Aylesbury, with support from the Paul Hamlyn Foundation, South East Museums Service and the Roald Dahl Foundation. It is an A4 booklet in eight topic sections, which correspond to the eight thematic displays in the ground floor of the museum.

Each topic is introduced on the left-hand page by a clear photograph of one or more of the objects on display, with a simple heading such as "Fossils" or "Farming". On the right hand page are six to eight lines of text which suggest things for the visitor to look at, listen to or do.

Touch the enormous tooth: this was from a real mammoth

What can you see in the display made of clay?

Above the printed text, which is in a deep blue 16 point type face using a clear font on white paper, are symbols to help those who have difficulty reading print. The symbols for "look" are used beside the photographs and also in the text as are the symbols for "touch" and "listen", and there is a sign for "go on" at the bottom of every right-hand page.

Purists could argue that the use of symbols is not consistent, either for grammatical words such as "the" and "for" which have symbols, and "as" which does not, or the object words like "wood" which has a symbol and "fossil" which does not. Given that the symbol system has not been developed for use in museums and there is obviously scope for improvement, Buckinghamshire County Museum deserve full credit for this innovative work to cater for people with learning disabilities.

Courtesy of Widgit Software

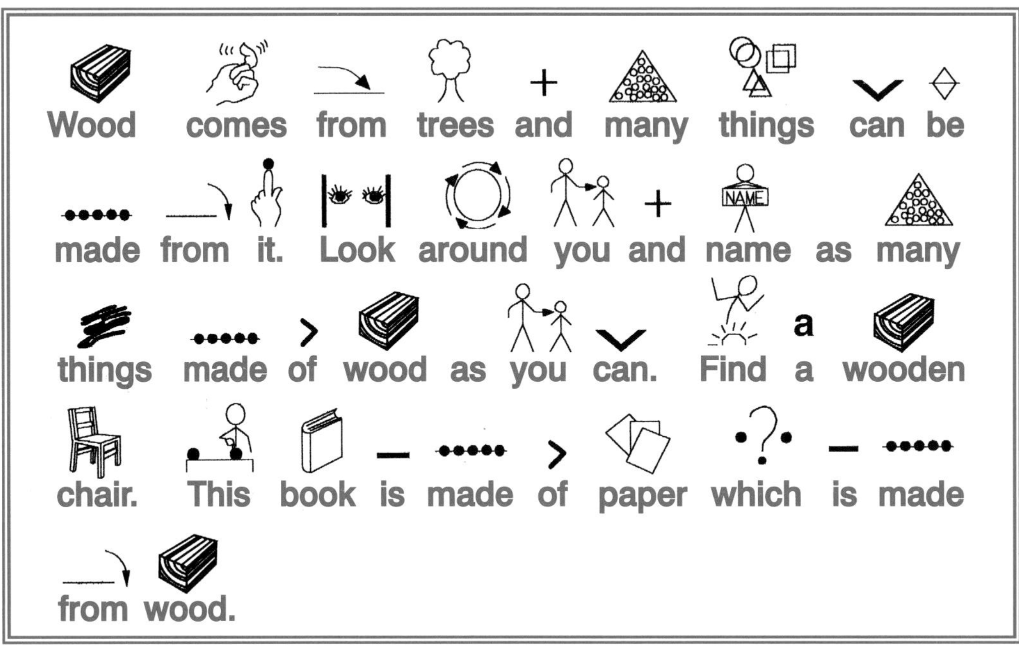

Gallery Interpretation

Interpretation should bring visitors closer to what they have come to see and encourage them to use their own eyes,
Marcus Binney *The Times* (05/06/96)[14]

The situation in galleries differs from that in museums, and is probably even further from outdoor interpretation. The Scottish Arts Council's *Guide to Interpretation*, quoted earlier, emphasises communication. Works of art are themselves a form of communication between the artist and the viewer in a way that an object never can be.

So in gallery interpretation the priority is to help the visitor respond to the work rather than to explain its importance, discuss the style or fit it into an art history context. These matters are relevant only in so far as they help the visitor to engage with the work displayed. SAC also make the point that interpretation is more difficult when the artist is still alive and has strong views about the presentation of his/her work.

A number of the works in the Modern British Art exhibition in the recently re-opened Tate Gallery in Liverpool have quotations by the artists alongside the conventional labels. These give visitors a different perspective on the works and an insight into the artist's intentions.

As public art galleries suffer almost more than museums from the 'it's not for the likes of us' syndrome, many have recognised the need for the entrance area to appear welcoming and make visitors feel at ease.

Comfortable spaces, chairs and rest areas signal a more inclusive and friendly approach to all.[15]

Such features are now included in the design of new galleries from an early stage, for example the new Arts Centre in Dundee and the planned Lowry Centre in Salford. Where a gallery is refurbished, the creation of a bright attractive entrance is an important asset in encouraging people to come in and explore further. An example of this is at the Laing Art Gallery in Newcastle, where the displays also have been made as accessible as possible.[16]

A fair amount of work has been done to make art more accessible for people with visual impairments, for example at Wolverhampton Museum and Art Gallery, Norwich Castle Museum and the National Portrait Gallery, London, but there are few references specifically to visitors with learning disabilities. Anne Pearson and Chitra Aloysius in *The Big Foot* refer to projects at the Dulwich Art Gallery and Sunderland Museum and Art Gallery, as well as responses to statues in the British Museum such as drawings and mimicking the poses. Anne Tynan's work[17] with pupils from special schools visiting the 16th and 17th century paintings at the Hunterian Art Gallery, Glasgow, includes pupils producing their own art, dressing up in period costume, listening to music of that time and creating a wheelchair dance.

Some galleries have tried to involve members of the public by asking for comments[18] or letting people choose works of art and have their comments used on the labels. One such was 'Women's Pictures' at Paisley Museum and Art Gallery. This exhibition:

showed the potential for emotional involvement with art exhibitions and argued that it was possible to break down the barriers associated with art.[19]

Many people would enjoy the experience of touch tours and learn from them. Most of us have had the experience of wishing that it

... in gallery interpretation the priority is to help the visitor respond to the work rather than to explain its importance, discuss the style or fit it into an art history context.

Changing Perceptions
Photograph by Sean Hudson

were possible to touch a sculpture because the material, wood, stone or metal, seems so inviting. Where touching is possible for all visitors, it is greatly appreciated as in *Changing Perceptions* in Edinburgh City Art Centre in 1997 and *See, Sense*, the version which toured Scotland in the *Travelling Gallery*.

INTACT was able to arrange a visit by a small group of young people with severe and multiple impairments to *Changing Perceptions*. They were spellbound by the light effects and fascinated by the varied textures of the stone sculptures.

Video is an interpretive method which has possibilities, recognised by Rebecca McGinnis, consultant on access, design and disability, speaking at the Fruitmarket Gallery Interpretation Seminar in November 1996. It is ...

... an accessible medium for people with all sorts of disabilities really, particularly people with a learning disability.[20]

While we have not seen video used by people with learning disabilities for access to interpretive information, it is certainly a powerful medium which they can relate to, as is shown by their response to video installations such as Dalziel and Scullion's *Endlessly* which was shown at the Scottish National Gallery of Modern Art in the summer of 1997. Where a gallery has shown a video of the artist(s) whose works are on display either at work, or talking about how these works came to be, visitors generally find this helpful.

When the National Gallery, London, toured George Stubbs' magnificent horse portrait, *Whistlejacket*, a video accompanied the picture. This showed close-ups of the mane, eye and tail, examples of classic sculpture showing horses in similar pose and film of modern racehorses in action. This added greatly to the enjoyment and knowledge of visitors and the well-designed accompanying leaflet/poster gave them the same information as the wall panels but in a form that they could hold to read at a suitable distance and take as a reminder of the exhibition.

Audio guides, mentioned earlier, have many advantages in galleries because they make it possible to listen and look at the same time. This cannot usually be done with text panels or labels because pictures are usually better seen from a reasonable distance, whereas labels tend to be quite small and require close-up reading. Understandably, gallery interpreters do not want to detract from the appearance of the works of art by using large and intrusive labels, so the visitor has to move back and forward. Audio guides avoid this problem.

The Liverpool Tate Gallery has static audio guides which are built into a small plinth. Visitors can choose to hear a number of options giving information about a nearby work. One of the most interesting of these was intended for partially sighted visitors. It directed attention to details of the sculpture in question which would be appreciated by everyone. The gallery hopes to be able to extend this system.

As well as audio guides, some galleries, such as the Louvre, Paris and the National Gallery, London, have produced CD-Roms for sale so that visitors who have suitable computers at home can obtain information about the collection. The National Gallery's 'Microgallery' allows visitors to explore areas of interest such as a particular artist, period or genre in a dedicated area and then obtain a print-out about the works they are interested in and directions on how to find them; effectively a personalised tour. Compact Disk-Interactive (CD-I) and HyperCard are other developments which give users control over the information they choose to access.

Live guides are liked by many visitors and are the most flexible way of providing information as they can respond directly to the needs of the individual visitor. The Fruitmarket Gallery's *Interpretive Pilot Project*[21] reported in June 1996 that visitors found them more comfortable and less intimidating than a formal tour. However real skill is required of the guide in judging when and how to approach a visitor. Some gallery guides, notably during a *Gallery Week* in March 1996, have worn large "Ask Me" badges to encourage visitors to approach them.

There are so many possible interpretation methods that galleries should be prepared to offer a variety of methods to suit different audience interests, abilities and learning styles. Accounts of some of them in use with people with learning disabilities will be dealt with in more detail in the section on the Galleries Pilot Project.

As the studies and visits mentioned show, children and adults with learning disabilities respond very naturally to works of art. They come to them without the preconceptions of more educated visitors and they are usually very perceptive in recognising emotion.

Note

Widgit Software for *Writing with Symbols* is available from Widgit Software, 102 Radford Road, Leamington Spa, CV3 1LF.

Audio guides have many advantages in galleries because they make it possible to listen and look at the same time.

References

1. *Museum Practice* Issue 5/Vol. 2 No. 2 (1997) Introduction to section devoted to Interpretation

2. *Interpreting Our Heritage* F Tilden **University of North Carolina Press** (1957)

3. *A Sense of Place* J Carter **Tourism and Environment Initiative** (1997)

4. *Museum Practice* op cit

5. *Issues of Museum Text* H Coxall in *Developing Museum Exhibitions for Lifelong Learning* edit G Durbin **GEM/Stationery Office** (1996)

6. *A Short Guide to Interpretation* M Cox **Scottish Arts Council Information Directory**

7. *Communicating generously* J Spalding *Museums Journal* (February 1992)

8. *Provoke, Relate, Reveal: a Policy Framework for Interpretation* **Scottish Natural Heritage**, Battleby, Redgorton, Perth (1997)

9. *Educators on Exhibit Teams: a New Role, a New Era* L Roberts in *Developing Museum Exhibitions for Lifelong Learning* edit G Durbin **GEM/Stationery Office** (1996)

10. **SNH** (1997) op cit

11. *Interpretive Master Planning* J Veverka **Falcon Press**, Montana (1994)

12. *Interpretation – A Guide* **The Association of Scottish Visitor Attractions (ASVA)**

13. *A Touch of Bucks – a Guide for People with Learning Disabilities*, **Buckinghamshire County Museum**, Aylesbury (1997)

14. M Binney *The Times* (05/06/96) quoted on the title page of The Fruitmarket Gallery *Interpretive Pilot Project Report*

15. **Cox** op cit

16. *Art History for all the family* paper by J Millard and D Phillips on the *Art on Tyneside* display at the Laing Art Gallery in Newcastle *Museums Journal* (February 1992)

17. *Let me show you,* Case Study by A Tynan in *Object Lessons* edit S Mitchell **SMC/HMSO** (1996)

18. *Permission to stick on labels* article on *Permission to speak* exhibition at Worcester City Museum and Art Gallery by D Dean *Museums Journal* (July 1996)

19. *Case Study: working with Women's Groups* by E Carnegie originally in *Scottish Museum News 8* (1992) reprinted in *Developing Museum Exhibitions for Lifelong Learning* edit G Durbin **GEM/Stationery Office** (1996)

20. *Making sense of Art* R McGinnis paper presented at the Fruitmarket Gallery *Interpretation* Seminar (November 1996)

21. *Interpretive Pilot Project* Report of June 1996 of the project at Edinburgh's Fruitmarket Gallery

Also consulted:

Site Interpretation: a Practical Guide **Scottish Tourist Board** (1993)

Principles of Countryside Interpretation and Interpretive Planning D Aldridge **Countryside Commission for Scotland/HMSO** (1975)

Picture this: *Museums Journal* (July 1996) articles on gallery interpretation at Manchester, Worcester, Swansea, Sheffield and Wolverhampton

Increasing the number of words decreases the number of readers Sandra Bicknell and Peter Mann *A Picture of Visitors for Exhibition Developers*.[1]

Given the amount of research on labels and signage that has already been undertaken in both commercial and academic contexts, it would be a pity not to take full account of it. There is no need to repeat information in detail which can be found elsewhere, but a number of problems can still cause difficulties mainly, though not only, for people with learning disabilities. It may also be useful to reiterate some of the recommendations which already exist, but are not always followed.

In museums and galleries throughout the world there are objects and images which can and should educate, excite and inspire. They give both pleasure and intellectual stimulus. But the quality and presentation of the text and labels at displays often fails to match the quality of the academic research or do justice to the objects themselves.

There are bad examples even in recently opened museums and galleries. Memorably, in one gallery (now changed) the light was so poor, the print so small and the labels so low that visitors were seen on their hands and knees trying to read them! In another, the arrangement of the label information about a collection of objects bore no logical relationship to the items in the case, which were not numbered.

Yet there are few objects which need no explanation or interpretation. Nearly everything in a display has to be explained and set in context by a label, whether or not graphics, audio guides or other devices are available. Good, succinct, legible labels are therefore a necessity for all visitors and not just for people with learning or visual disabilities or poor literacy.

Despite the general perception that access for disabled people is about providing ramps for wheelchairs, the reality is that there is a far greater problem in providing access for people with learning disabilities, poor literacy or visual impairment. In other words, legible signs are more important, and will help more people, than is generally realised.

Some statistics[2] will help illustrate the size of the potential market of beneficiaries.

While an estimated 1 million people in the UK have learning disabilities, there are over 7 million adults with literacy problems (one survey by the Basic Skills Agency suggests that as many as 11% of the population have poor or below average literacy skills). There are also 1.7 million people with visual impairments which prevent them reading standard print easily and around 10 million who have some problems with mobility, some resulting from ageing. Those affected may tire quickly and have difficulty in bending or stretching.

At present there are about 9 million elderly people in the UK, and this number is growing. In 1951, 1 in 10 of the population was over 65: by 2021 it will be 1 in 5, i.e. 10.9 million people. Visual deterioration is intrinsically linked to the ageing process and about 45% of the UK population require glasses or contact lenses. As we age the lens of the eye begins to yellow. Older readers see less contrast between colours and need higher light levels. Moreover, 1 in 12 of men have some degree of colour blindness (predominantly red/green).

Museums must also attract visitors of different nationalities and varying educational standards. This means that, ideally, information on labels should be comprehensible by people for whom English is not the first language as well as

In one gallery (now changed) the light was so poor, the print so small and the labels so low that visitors were seen on their hands and knees trying to read them!

More legible labels, with good contrast, would help all museum visitors and not just those with visual impairment or literacy problems.

Accessibility begins as a mandate to serve people who have been discriminated against for centuries; it prevails as a tool that serves diverse audiences for a lifetime.[3]

by people with below average literacy. This does not imply either over simplification or being patronising: it just means the admittedly difficult task of conveying accurate information in a way that is readily understood by people with only basic literacy in English. The Plain English Campaign has led the way in the field of clear communication. This is about writing clearly without being patronising or over-simple.

Anne Pearson, now of the Metropolitan Museum of Art in New York, Dr Jan Walmsley of the School of Health and Social Welfare, the Open University, and Janice Majewski of the Smithsonian Institution, Washington, along with many others, argue strongly that more legible labels, with good contrast, would help all museum visitors and not just those with visual impairment or literacy problems. For example, the Smithsonian Guidelines say:

> Discovering exciting, attractive ways to make exhibitions accessible will most directly serve people with disabilities and older adults. But to name an audience who will not benefit by these designs is impossible. Accessibility begins as a mandate to serve people who have been discriminated against for centuries; it prevails as a tool that serves diverse audiences for a lifetime.[3]

In *Arts for Everyone*, Anne Pearson argues:

> Lettering on labels should be much clearer. Many sighted museum visitors, as well as the visually handicapped, would benefit from greater clarity ... There should be a greater contrast with the background instead of the current fashion for lettering to be in subtle colours which merge into the background ... Labels should be set at a slight angle, 45 degrees, and preferably at eye level, and not on the back wall of deep display cases or too low for normal adult reading.[4]

The Metropolitan Museum of Art say that:

> larger, easier-to-read type and labels with simple text will be more accessible to visitors with lower comprehension levels (including individuals with developmental disabilities). In fact, most museum visitors should benefit from the implementation of these standards ... And easily accessible labels and signs will enhance the museum experience for adults over sixty-five who may have some degree of vision, hearing or mobility impairment as a result of the ageing process.[5]

We must ensure that the quality and legibility of the labels in new displays do justice to the quality of the objects. It would be quite inexcusable for us to be faced in the new millennium with complaints that enjoyment of the educational and cultural wealth of displays in our museums and galleries is spoiled because people can neither find their way to the gallery they want, nor read the labels when they get there.

At the end of this section are guidelines which refer to typefaces, print size and position.

Design of Labels and Text Panels

At the risk of stating the obvious, the purpose of labels is to convey information, not to make design statements in themselves.

Labels which feature, say, red text on a pink background or green on grey or which have text struggling to be deciphered over a background graphic are simply not fit for their purpose. One recent display has light green text on a grey background and compounds the felony by putting the text on a thick, translucent plate so that the text throws shadows of itself! In another, the text has been printed straight on to the glass of a cased display, so that the visitor has to try to read it through surface reflections and against a changing background of differently coloured, shaped and sized objects in the case itself.

Of course graphics are important: they can help interpret the objects. But they should normally be free-standing and not a confusing background to large chunks of text. Curators should have the last word on accuracy of content, and educators the last word on legibility, readability and comprehension.

There are many complaints that labels are difficult to read by people who have bifocals, because the print is too small to be read at a distance yet the visitor cannot get close enough to the label to use the reading lenses. The position of lights in relation to labels is also crucial. A recent exhibition had some labels which were virtually unreadable because the reader cast his or her own shadow on the label! In another, a vertical light directly over a vertical label illuminated only the centre of the top few lines.

Amount of Information

information overload causes distortion and fatigue John Veverka *Interpretive Master Planning*[6]

Veverka believes that if a label is more than 50 words long, it probably will not be read. He recommends that language should be used sparingly and jargon or technical terms avoided.

Eric Kentley and Dick Negus in *Writing on the wall: a guide for presenting exhibition text*[7] suggest that all writing should be:

- clear
- concise
- relevant
- consistent
- enthusiastic

To achieve consistency, they suggest an intelligible information-structure for the basic types of written information-carriers

- Titles – main and section
- Introductory panels – main and section
- Group captions
- Didactic panels
- Object captions
- Multi-object captions

They suggest that, while every exhibition will not require all of these, the information structure should be part of the design process with the location and purpose of each element defined.

A hierarchy of information both across several interpretation methods, and within the domain of text has already been referred to in the section on interpretation. Many visitors would like to be able to decide quickly whether a gallery, an area, a display case or a single object is something that they want to find out more about so that they can determine whether or not to invest time in looking more closely. It is also

... the purpose of labels is to convey information, not to make design statements in themselves.

A good example of an interpretive panel with hierarchy of text and illustrations by Historic Scotland

important that they should not be put off by dauntingly long sections of writing with little white space. Many people are deterred by this and will not even start to read, whereas they might consider reading a few small, clearly spaced sections.

Helen Coxall in *Writing for Different Audiences*[8] suggests starting with the most important points, not leaving them to the end. This technique is familiar to newspaper readers who are able to grasp the main idea from the headline, the most important points in the first paragraph and the details in the rest of the article. An equivalent system for museum text would benefit all visitors.

Such a hierarchy could cater for a wide variety of audiences: people with poor literacy, casual 'browser', interested tourist or serious student, with each visitor able to choose the level of information s/he wants.

The particular concern of the INTACT project is of course the need to attract and serve people who have learning or communication disabilities: a very large potential market (1 million in the UK with a market potential, according to Mencap, of £1.65 billion). While we cannot expect that all labels in all displays can be made accessible to people with learning disabilities, we are convinced (and are supported by expert opinion) that attempts to make displays more accessible to people with learning disabilities will in practice help everyone.

Content of Labels and Text Panels

Text should be relevant to visitors' experience if they are to understand it.
Gammon & Moussouri (1995)[9]

Content has already been mentioned in passing, but for people with learning disabilities, simple jargon-free language is essential. The use of active verbs, personal language and ways of relating information to things people know about, such as expressing a height in terms of double-decker buses, are all good ways of engaging peoples' interest.

It has been suggested that curators are the worst people to write information about the objects they wish to display as they are, by their very work, too close to them, and may not appreciate how little the non-expert visitor may know. While this is too sweeping, as the curator's knowledge is essential, there is a real skill in providing information in a way which is academically respectable, easily understood and well expressed.

The article in *Museum Practice 5* on *Display Text* suggests that for general audiences it is common practice to aim at a reading age of 12 or 13 for introductory text and up to 15 for subsequent levels. We mentioned earlier the aim of the Museum of Scotland which is that 50% – messages, objects, text and information technology where appropriate – should be capable of being understood by the average 10 year old.

There are a number of 'readability' tests, including some wordprocessing software which will check this. However they should be treated with caution. James Carter in *How **old** is this Text?*[10] mentions two of these tests but warns of a computer package which rejected "dragon" and "dinosaur". He says:

tests like these are no substitute for writing with feeling and power. Writing solely to match a particular reading age could easily be dull: the trick is to write simply but with an enthusiasm that makes your writing worth reading.

Beverly Serrell, in *Exhibit Labels – An Interpretive Approach*[11], an excellent and detailed reference book, suggests that the right reading level is aimed at the majority of visitors, not at either the lowest or the highest common denominator. She says:

Appeal to the would-be readers – people who will read if the label is short enough, if it looks easy to read, if it is legible and if they have time. Visitors are more likely to take the time to read if a label looks like it is written for them.

Some of the reasons why visitors ignore labels are mentioned in Hirschi and Screven's *Effects of Questions on Visitor Reading Behaviour*.[12] They are:

- location
- length
- wording
- failure to anticipate visitors' existing levels of knowledge

They suggest that the use of questions can support label reading and motivate visitors to read more or to look at an adjacent label and to study the objects more closely to work out the answer. The results of their research, which consisted of observing family groups, were that the areas with questions got more visitor attention than those without. However, the visitors tended to focus on a narrow range of information related to the specific questions. Serrell suggests that the best questions are those that visitors themselves ask and quotes an example which asks *"How heavy is a hippo?"* and answers this under a flap with a cartoon of children piled on the end of a see-saw and the caption, "As heavy as eighty 12-year-olds".[13]

Paulette McManus in *Label Reading Behaviour* notes that when visitors are in groups or couples, it is common for one person to read out at least some of the information, and that this may elicit questions or comments from companions. Label reading is social behaviour. Just as they talk to each other, visitors ...

... interpret texts in an interactive manner ... they approach the exhibit within a communicative framework which includes the exhibition team.[14]

Visitors often react as if the team is talking to them through the exhibit and they may voice their reactions to it and to the display text. Using active verbs and personal language ("you", "we") encourages this dialogue which adds to the visitor's sense of belonging.

A number of museums and galleries have tried asking visitors to write labels. The Laing Art Gallery in Newcastle has invited various community groups to come in, look at some pictures or ceramics in store and put them in a display *From the Vaults* with information supplied by the people who chose the works. Kelvingrove Art Gallery and Museum have a *Visitors' Choice*, where people can choose a picture from the promenade area, which is then given star billing for a month, with the visitor's explanation of why it was chosen.

The National Museums of Scotland set up a *Junior Board* to advise on how to make sure that the new Museum of Scotland is an exciting and interesting place for children. It consists of twelve pupils, aged 9 – 14, selected from schools all over Scotland. They are writing labels for fifty Museum of Scotland objects which are also being featured in the Children's Guide to the new Museum.

There are already Junior Board labels in the Art and Industry Gallery in the Royal Museum (see following page) which are enjoyed by many visitors who like the personal approach.

... people will read if the label is short enough, if it looks easy to read, if it is legible and if they have time. Visitors are more likely to take the time to read if a label looks like it is written for them.

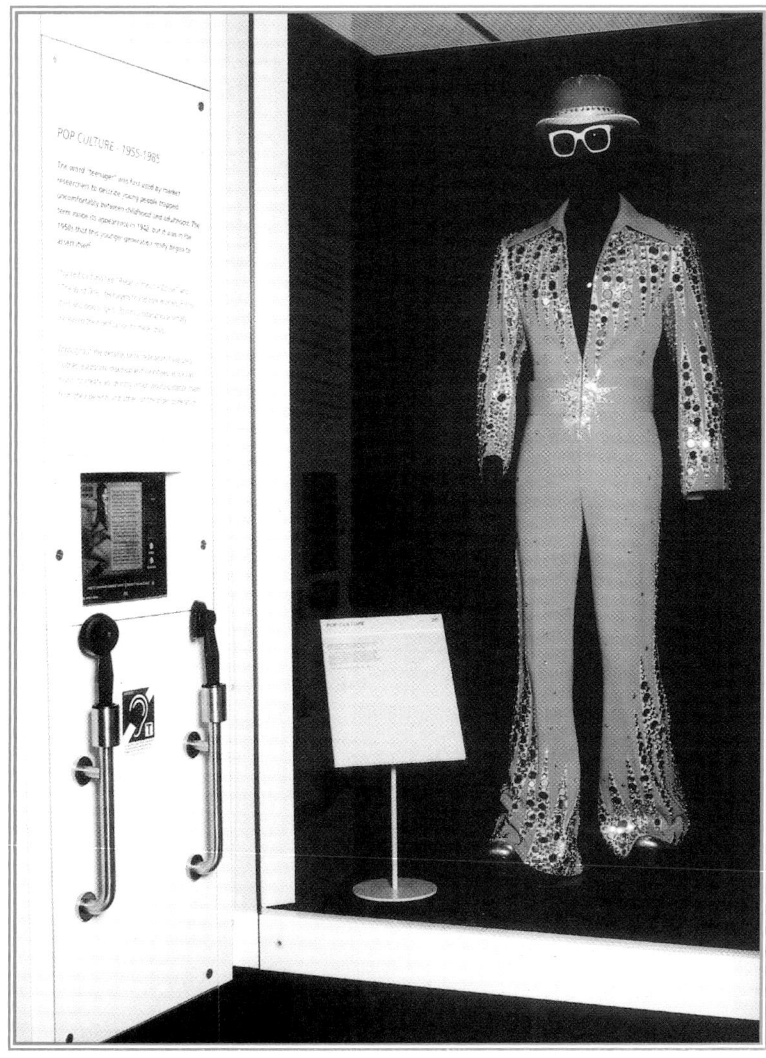

Elton John's suit in the Royal Museum of Scotland and the associated information panels.

ELTON JOHN'S OUTFIT:
Amy Bannister (Age 12)

Wow, what an outfit! It's hard to imagine pop star Elton John as he is now parading this suit when he was on tour in 1972. My brother who is a devoted Elton John fan was ecstatic when he saw this classic suit, but admitted even he would find it hard to wear in today's fashion scene. The big question is, would you?

20 POP CULTURE

JUMP SUIT, BOWLER HAT, TINTED SPECTACLES AND BOOTS, Crimplene, silvered leather, mirror glass, white plastic, diamanté and machine embroidery.

This outfit was first worn on the Muppet Show and then on tour. The singer liked it so much he had it copied in green the following year. In a very exaggerated form it shows the main features of street fashion in the early 1970s. The designer is a celebrated Hollywood figure, who has also created costumes for the Supremes, Tina Turner and Cher.

Designed by Bob Mackie for Elton John; 1972.

Signage

Orientation in many big museums could be improved. How often do we see visitors come into an entrance hall only to stop, at a loss where to go. Although floor plans may be readily available in large museums, many visitors still have to ask how to find the toilets or the café.

According to Steven Bitgood's *Visitor Orientation and Circulation: Some General Principles*[15] there are three major areas:

1. conceptual orientation
2. visitor circulation
3. wayfinding

The first is important because visitors tend to have a more satisfying experience if they know where to go, what to expect, how long a visit will take and how to find the comfort facilities: toilets, cafeterias and seating areas.

The second discusses principles such as visitors tending to go to landmarks, the closest visible object, where other people are, and entering or exiting when they encounter a door.

On the last he recommends that wayfinding information should be placed where it is needed at critical choice points, that it should be easily seen, and that duplicated (ie repeated in different formats) information should be provided to decrease the chance of its being missed, with a variety of methods such as floor plans, direction signs, and/or orientation maps with "You are here" signs.

Anyone with an interest in this topic should read for themselves Steven Bitgood's short but comprehensive account of the principles of orientation.

These general principles are as valid for people with learning disabilities as for the general visitor. In addition, learning disabled visitors would be helped by large clear print with symbols or logos where appropriate, and colour coding, but these would also help many other people including visitors whose first language is not English.

The Glasgow School of Art has done work on this and points to airport terminals, and the new Buchanan Bus station in Glasgow as models of clear direction, good orientation for large numbers of visitors and excellent use of symbols or icons.

The Metropolitan Museum, New York says in its draft *Standards Manual for Signs and Labels*:

signs that feature symbols, pictographs and photographs will be more readily understood by non-English speaking visitors [16]

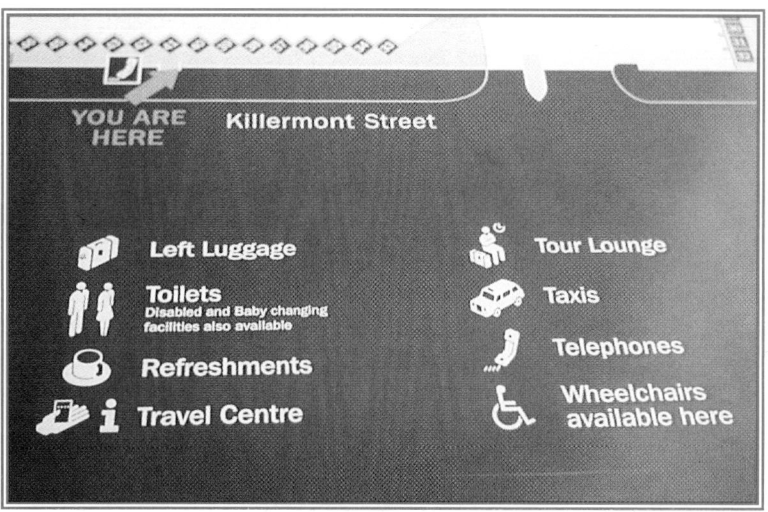

Sign at Buchanan Bus Station in Glasgow

In *Signs, Symbols and Icons* [17] Sassoon and Gaur deal in detail with icons and their history. They argue that old icons worked successfully because the designer and the reader lived within the same community: both had access to a pool of shared experience. This is no longer the case. While, therefore, in an ideal world there should be a single, simple system of symbols or icons which would be universally accepted as representing toilets, café, lift, information, tickets, left luggage etc., in practice no system exists. To take one obvious example, the Western convention of representing male and female toilets by figures in trousers and skirts is the precise opposite of the customary dress of men and women in some Eastern countries!

Some conventions are universally understood, for example the running figure and arrow for "Emergency Exit", and the "No Entry" sign. We should certainly try to make more use of symbols and icons, and less use of words, in helping our visitors to find their way around. Symbols are more likely to reinforce than to replace words.

A combination of short words and symbols is likely in practice to offer the best solution.

Signs should also be easily located. For visually impaired people, the first problem is to locate the sign so they should be placed in a logical position and be obviously identifiable. The RNIB recommend that the sign board should contrast with the background against which it is seen and the lettering should contrast with the sign board.[18]

In *Something to see, Something to do, Somewhere to sit*[19] Jayne Earnescliffe says:

When questioned about signposting, some visitors had not noticed any, and others complained that information was illegible because of small lettering, crowded text or complexity of design. Easily recognised symbols, such as a plate, knife and fork to indicate the café, are a concise, useful way of conveying a lot of information.

Clearly there is room for improvement in many institutions. Carefully designed, legible floor plans along with better signs and icons for facilities such as toilets, lifts and cafés would help all visitors. They must also be readily apparent ... It should be possible to design and locate attractive signs and means of orientation which do not detract from the ambience of the building.

Notes

1. This does not present the results of original research by INTACT. Many people have done much work on legibility, in both academic and commercial contexts, and we have simply attempted to bring together the results of work by many others.

2. Anyone writing labels is recommended to read the excellent article *Display Text* in *Museum Practice* Issue 5 (Vol. 2, No. 2) (1997) and Beverley Serrell's *Exhibit Labels – an Interpretive Approach*. Both discuss categories of text, content, style and language.

Guidelines

Although this note does not pretend to be comprehensive or definitive, and does not claim to have drawn on all published work on legibility, there seems to be a consensus emerging on the following points:

1. **A hierarchy of information** should be offered, from short headlines to computer data bases.

2. **Labels should be at a height, distance and angle which enables them to be read by people in wheelchairs and by people wearing bi-focals.** The Metropolitan Museum of Art base their minimum standards of type size on a viewing distance of not more than 46 cm. from the label or sign, installed at the optimal height. It follows that people with bi-focals will have difficulty in reading a label at the back or foot of a display case.

3. **Clear contrast between type and background is fundamental.** Pastel shades or yellow ink must never be used, and lettering should not be superimposed on a background graphic. Some argue that a background graphic can be acceptable provided the contrast between text and background is at least 70%, but even then the text should be confined to a brief heading in very bold type and should not extend to a detailed description. Pale colours on a coloured background (e.g. grey on blue or light green on grey) should be avoided. Colours that can be confused by people with colour blindness (red, brown, orange, yellow and green) should be avoided. Reversal, for example white on black, can be acceptable, but not if it is in small type and not for long passages: continuous reversed-out text is tiring to read at any size.

4. **Labels should not use a reflective surface** such as a metal plate or enamel paint, and must be lit without shadows being thrown by objects, other labels or the readers themselves.

5. Right justification should not be used. Text justified on the left margin only is easier to read because it allows more even spacing of words. Hyphenation of words at the end of lines reduces legibility and reading speed (*Museum Practice 5* p. 65). Fitting text into an unusual shape, such as a shield outline or around a picture, is not recommended.

6. Boxes and bullet points can be helpful.

7. Informality, such as a question and answer format, can help engage attention. Technical terms and jargon should be avoided or explained. The Conservation Centre in Liverpool has good examples both of question and answer and of a glossary of words which are unusual or are used in a specialised sense.

8. Fancy typefaces should not be used. That includes italics, except to distinguish quotations, for a brief title or for emphasis. Extra bold type can be counter-productive because it can run letters too close for clarity.

9. A mixture of upper and lower case is easier to read than a panel of all upper case, because people get their reading cues from the peaks and troughs of the letters.

10. There is a difference of view about serif (type which uses small strokes to finish off letters) versus sans serif, but there is complete unanimity about the need for a simple, clear type face. Most agree that it is preferable to use either sans serif, such as Univers or Helvetica, or a simple or modified serif type such as Century Schoolbook or Times Roman. Participants in a Label Study carried out by the Metropolitan Museum rated Helvetica highest.

11. Paragraphs should be well spaced and 50 to 55 characters is a good line length. The Basic Skills Agency emphasise the importance of 'white space' and 'leading' (the spacing between lines). Too close, and the hesitant reader will tend to drop lines: too far apart, and the reader will not be clear whether the lines relate to each other at all. Obviously, leading depends on type size, but with 12 point type, a leading of 14 or 16 point is recommended. Similarly, 'tracking' (the space between letters) should be adequate. The Metropolitan Museum of Art Guidelines say that text without sufficient letter and word spacing is more difficult to read because the letters and words begin to run together. For a person with low vision, the white space around a letter is as important as the letter itself.

12. Labels in cases should relate clearly to objects by a logical, consistent numbering or mapping system.

13. There are recommendations on text size and reading distance by the National Maritime Museum in London, the Metropolitan Museum of Art in New York, and also in *Museum Practice 5*. In her *Practical Guide* Gail Nolan suggests that a minimum type size of 18 to 36 point is suitable for most exhibition labels, but main texts on introductory labels should be considerably larger, around 48 point. *Museum Practice* recommends type size of 18 points at a maximum viewing distance of 700mm and 36 points at a maximum of 1,400mm.

14. There should be consistent location of labels. The Metropolitan Museum say that wall labels should be centred at 137 cm from the floor (this ties in neatly with the *Museum Practice* recommendation of 140cm) while case labels attached to the outside of the case (only when absolutely necessary) should be at a height of between 91 cm and 122 cm and at an angle of between 30 and 45 degrees.

15. Numerals need care. Many people with low vision can easily misread the numerals ...

3 5 6 8 9 0

... when the tails curl over.

References

1. *A Picture of Visitors for Exhibition Developers* S Bicknell and P Mann (1993) reprinted in *Developing Museum Exhibitions for Lifelong Learning* edit G Durbin **GEM/Stationery Office** (1996)

2. Statistics from Appendix to *The Informability Manual* W Gregory **HMSO** (1996)

3. *Accessible Exhibition Design* J Majewski **Smithsonian Institution** Washington (1996)

4. *Arts for Everyone* A Pearson **Carnegie UK Trust** (1985)

5. *Standards Manual for Signs and Labels* **Metropolitan Museum of Art** New York (draft 1995)

6. *Interpretive Master Planning* J Veverka **Falcon Press** Montana (1994)

7. *Writing on the Wall: a Guide for presenting exhibition text* E Kentley and D Negus **National Maritime Museum** (1989)

8. *Writing for Different Audiences* H Coxall (1991) reprinted in *Developing Museum Exhibitions for Lifelong Learning* edit G Durbin **GEM/Stationery Office** (1996)

9. *Text and Labels – How to make them readable* B Gammon and T Moussouri **The Science Museum** London (October 1995)

10. *How **old** is this text?* J Carter **Environmental Interpretation** (Feb 1993)

11. *Exhibit Labels – an Interpretive Approach* B Serrell **Altamira** (1996)

12. *Effects of Questions on Visitor Reading Behaviour* K D Hirschi and C Screven (1988) reprinted in *Developing Museum Exhibitions for Lifelong Learning* edit G Durbin **GEM/Stationery Office** (1996)

13. **Serrell** (1996) op cit

14. *Label Reading Behaviour* P McManus (1989) reprinted in *Developing Museum Exhibitions for Lifelong Learning* edit G Durbin **GEM/Stationery Office** (1996)

15. *Visitor Orientation and Circulation: some general principles,* S Bitgood (1992) reprinted in *Developing Museum Exhibitions for Lifelong Learning* edit G Durbin **GEM/Stationery Office** (1996)

16. **Metropolitan Museum of Art** New York (draft 1995) op cit

17. *Signs, Symbols and Icons* Sassoon and Gaur **Intellect Books** (1997)

18. *Building Sight* RNIB London **HMSO** (1997)

19. *Something to see, Something to do, Somewhere to sit* J Earnescliffe *Museum Practice 4* (1997)

Additional Sources

G Nolan *Practical Guide to designing Exhibitions to include people with disabilities* **NMS** (1997)

J Gill *Access Prohibited? Information for Designers of Public Access Terminals*

The Basic Skills Agency

The Plain English Campaign *How to write reports in plain English* Manchester (1995)

People First

The Glasgow School of Art A Macdonald and D Frier Product Design Department

The Conservation Centre, National Museums and Galleries on Merseyside

Millhouse Graphics for the Museum of Scotland

The Institute of Grocery Distribution who have to resolve the conflict between the legal need to give more information to the consumer and the need to keep it simple and legible (and to whom impact and legibility means money!)

The Disabled Visitor R Denman and S Clarkson **English Tourist Board Insights** (1991)

How not to do it!

Clear contrast between type and background is fundamental. Pastel shades or yellow ink must never be used, and lettering should not be superimposed on a background graphic. Some argue that a background graphic can be acceptable provided the contrast between text and background is at least 70%, but even then the text should be confined to a brief heading in very bold type and should not extend to a detailed description.

Pale colours on a coloured background (e.g. grey on blue or light green on grey) should be avoided.

Colours that can be confused by people with colour blindness (red, brown, orange, yellow and green) should be avoided. Reversal, for example white on black, can be acceptable, but not if it is in small type and not for long passages: continuous reversed-out text is tiring to read [illegible]

Right justification should not be used. Text justified on the left margin only is easier to read because it allows more even spacing of words. Hyphenation of words at the end of lines reduces legibility and reading speed (Museum Practice p. 65). Fitting text into an unusual shape, such as a shield outline or around a picture, is not recommended.

Fancy type faces should not be used. That includes italics, except to distinguish quotations, for a brief title or for emphasis.

Extra bold type can be counter-productive because it can run letters too close for clarity.

A MIXTURE OF UPPER AND LOWER CASE IS EASIER TO READ THAN A PANEL OF ALL UPPER CASE, BECAUSE PEOPLE GET THEIR READING CUES FROM THE PEAKS AND TROUGHS OF THE LETTERS.

Paragraphs should be well spaced and 50 to 55 characters is a good line length. The Basic Skills Agency emphasise the importance of 'white space' and 'leading' (the spacing between lines). Too close, and the hesitant reader will tend to drop lines: too far apart, and the reader will not be clear whether the lines relate to each other at all. Obviously, leading depends on type size, but with 12 point type, a leading of 14 or 16 point is recommended. Similarly, 'tracking' (the space between letters) should be adequate. The Metropolitan Museum of Art Guidelines say that text without sufficient letter and word spacing is more difficult to read because the letters and words begin to run together. For a person with low vision, the white space around a letter is as important as the letter itself.

Introduction

The eight pilot projects were set up in order to test in practice some of the ideas which came from the research. We wanted to find out how feasible these were when tested in a real situation and to get feedback from museum staff and from visitors with learning disabilities, along with carers, where this was possible.

To make the exercise as wide ranging as possible, it was decided early on to have these pilot projects in a number of locations throughout Scotland and to try to include different types and sizes of museums, as well as art galleries and at least one historic site.

In some cases the places selected themselves because there were people interested in taking part who had suggestions of their own which we were then able to take up. However this meant that the different groups involved in the exercise often had their own agendas. At times, it became a balancing act to try to fulfil all of the requirements.

All these projects were co-operative ventures which, in most cases, included three very different agendas:

- those of INTACT
- those of the museum(s) and/or Gallery/ies
- those of the people with learning disabilities and the organisations representing them.

This has meant that a lot of negotiation took place so that all the parties felt that they 'owned' the project and that they all would gain something from it.

Obviously such negotiation took time, particularly when consulting the wishes of people with learning disabilities who need time to consider what is involved and to express their needs and preferences in a supportive environment. The projects had to be planned, agreed, tried out and evaluated, then conclusions had to be drawn up. While at times this could be frustrating, in retrospect the experience was valuable in demonstrating that some things are better not rushed. It is better to listen to and respect the views of those concerned rather than to try to steamroller something through, just because we thought it was a good idea.

Our front-end evaluation for each of the pilot projects was based on preliminary consultation with people with learning disabilities and their carers as well as discussions with museum staff. In many cases, the project was modified as it progressed as we responded to comments and suggestions. Finally, we asked the opinions of the participants on how successful we had been.

While a statistical evaluation was not possible because of the small numbers of people involved, it was heartening to receive the positive feedback we did. Wherever possible, actual comments have been quoted to back up what might otherwise seem rather subjective.

It will be obvious in reading the accounts of these pilot projects that they did not all proceed as expected, and some of the findings were not what we had set out to look at. The reports are intended to be fair to all participants, even when the results were not necessarily what we had wanted, and the participants have been consulted to ensure that they are happy with the account. Whatever the outcome of these pilots, we have learnt a great deal – possibly more in the case of those which did not go according to plan than in those that did.

Audio guides can liberate visitors from reading labels and have the capacity to provide them with optional layers of information and contextual material under their direct control. *Museum Practice 5* (1997)

Historic Scotland offered funding to INTACT, on the understanding that one of the pilot projects would be in one of their properties, perhaps focusing on audio guides. This also met with our own wish to extend the work outside the Central Belt of Scotland. Following discussions about which would be the most appropriate of their sites, Jedburgh Abbey emerged as one where Historic Scotland were planning to upgrade their interpretation.

INTACT's partners:

Chris Tabraham
Principal Inspector of Ancient Monuments
Historic Scotland

Doreen Grove
Inspector of Ancient Monuments
Historic Scotland

Marion Fry
Education Officer, Historic Scotland

Rowland Duncan
Custodian at Jedburgh Abbey

Shona McMillan
Arts and Communication Technology (ACT)
now Antenna Audio Manager Scotland

David Shapero
ACT/Antenna Audio Technical Manager

Christianne Bakker
ACT/Antenna Audio Tour Music Production

Alasdair Hutton
Jedburgh script narrator

Using an Audio Guide at Jedburgh Abbey

Staff and members
Millside Centre, Galashiels

Staff and members
Katherine Elliot Centre, Hawick

Staff and members
Lanark Lodge Centre, Duns

Mary Daykin
People First co-ordinator

Aims

Historic Scotland's Aims:

- to improve access to Jedburgh Abbey for people with learning or communication disabilities in a way which would get across the main messages about the site and fit in with existing methods of interpretation

- to learn more about ways of improving access for people with learning disabilities in general so that some of what is learnt at Jedburgh can be applied at other Historic Scotland sites

INTACT's Aims:

- to improve access to information about the site for people with learning and communication disabilities

- (which emerged as the project progressed) to explore the use of audio guides as a way of doing this

- (following from the above) to gain experience of producing scripts for people with learning disabilities which will prove useful in producing them for a 6 month trial at the Museum of Scotland when it opens

The Process

Jedburgh Abbey is just nine miles from the English border, with the abbey church on a ridge and the remains of the monastic buildings on a south-facing slope down to a channel of the Jed Water. The former cloister garden has been restored with the kinds of plants there would have been when the Augustinian canons lived there. An exhibition of carved stones is in a building by the west door and the picnic area has old fruit trees such as medlar and a 'Jeddart' pear.

One disadvantage of the sloping site is that it is not possible to make it accessible for wheel chair users, and even those with quite mild mobility problems could find the many steps and changes of level difficult. However, when Historic Scotland built the Visitor Centre, level access was provided to the upper storey of this and to a platform giving an excellent view of the complex.

On this upper floor is a display area which includes a model of the whole abbey and church showing what the buildings would have been like about 500 years ago when it was inhabited by canons of the Augustinian order. This is in front of a huge window looking out at the Abbey as it is today. By this window is a model figure of one of these "black canons" in his robes, and there is a beautiful collection of early Christian stone carvings. A display case houses a carved walrus ivory comb, a lamp and other objects found during the excavations of the building foundations in 1984. The video, which shows life in a modern abbey to give visitors an idea of the kind of life led by the canons, is on the lower floor as is the shop.

Around the site are seven viewpoints with information panels about what can be seen from each. These are well presented with the main ideas in large text, usually telling visitors about the function of each area and a highlighted sketch plan showing how that area fits into the whole. Often additional information is given in smaller writing. The same information is also translated into German, French, Italian and Spanish, though this is in a much reduced typeface.

However, this information, good though it is, has limited uses for those who are not confident readers. A multi-sensory approach would be possible if audio guides were used to give the main information on the written panels, as some of the stone carvings could be touched and the herbs scent the cloister garden in the summer.

Approaches were made to Marion Fry, Historic Scotland's Education Officer, and Doreen Grove, the Inspector of Ancient Monuments responsible for Jedburgh. Historic Scotland were already planning to update the interpretive panels at Jedburgh so that there would be a more obvious hierarchy of information, along with pictures and diagrams as at present. This would make it easier for people who wished to read only the basic information.

Marion Fry provided a copy of a workbook which had been devised for school pupils, but did not have contacts with special needs teachers in the Borders area at that time. Possibilities discussed included audio guides and some of the ideas in the pupils' guide which pointed out particular features of the building.

In order to get advice from people with learning disabilities and those who worked with them, it was agreed that Marion would set up a meeting with some special needs teachers and INTACT would follow up contacts with day centres and People First, the advocacy organisation for people with learning disabilities which has a branch in the Borders.

Through this last contact, a small group of people with learning disabilities from Duns came to the Abbey along with a co-ordinator. After watching the video which everyone enjoyed though they found some of the language and ideas difficult (for example, 'celibacy'), we all walked round the site. Apart from the Abbey Church, where the columns and arches are well preserved, the group found the ruins difficult to understand. One man could read a bit, but was put off by the amount of writing on the panels and would have liked more drawings to explain things.

The group required a lot of explanation as we went round but were interested to know what the different parts of the abbey had been used for. They were struck by the fact that the canons who lived there had to get up to pray in the middle of the night. They were all intrigued by what they saw but used little of the written information, and sometimes found the language too difficult even when read out.

Everyone managed the stairs up to the gallery at the west end of the church and were very impressed with the view from there. They also liked being able to touch some of the carved stones.

Following the visit, the co-ordinator sent feedback on the reactions of the group. The very positive message was that they all enjoyed the site and had got a lot out of the visit. The main problem was access to easily understood information as the language on the video and on the information panels was too difficult on the whole, for example, 'lofty', 'radical alteration' or 'frugal meals'. However they had learned something of the life of the abbey, helped by the visual clues on the video and the drawings on the information boards and by looking at details of the site itself.

This suggested that providing information through a variety of means was the most successful method of helping people with learning disabilities to find out about a site like Jedburgh Abbey. A very simple, illustrated guide might help, as would an audio guide in simple language. The best would be someone who could explain things to people with learning disabilities as they went round and answer their questions, but this is not often possible.

This information was passed to Historic Scotland along with comments on other sites at Melrose Abbey and Arbroath Abbey. A meeting at Jedburgh with two teachers in special education, one from a primary school and one from a secondary, took place and was very helpful. Doreen and Marion were present and explained some of Historic Scotland's plans. Marion hoped to be able to create more space for school and other groups to work; the possibilities included some 'hands-on' experience with some of the less valuable stones, an arch-building exercise with shaped, lightweight 'stones', replica canons' robes and drama activities.

It was intended to upgrade and simplify the wall panels in the Visitor Centre and the information panels at the viewpoints. The display of the stones housed in the building behind the west door could be improved to include information about the technology needed to build such a structure in the 12th century and show the templates and tools used. It was hoped that there would still be some stones which visitors could touch.

The teachers made a number of suggestions about the information boards including more drawings of what the canons would be doing in the various areas, simplifying the language, breaking the information into smaller paragraphs and taking away the right justification which made the text too 'blocky'. They also suggested captions for the video and the possibility that teachers could "pause" it so that they could talk about some of the difficult concepts with their groups. Some concerns were expressed about encouraging people to touch the herbs in the herb garden as a number of the plants might possibly cause skin irritation.

While there was no shortage of ideas, some would take time to develop. With the INTACT timetable of a two year project, by now into the second year, the decision was made to produce a script for a short audio guide which would be suitable for people with learning disabilities but which would also help the many members of the general public who are not confident readers, or who simply prefer to get information in audio form.

Meanwhile, INTACT had received support from the Viscount Nuffield Auxiliary Fund of the Nuffield Foundation for an audio guide trial and three firms who produced audio-guides were approached. After some negotiation, the tender from Arts Communication and Technology (ACT), now Antenna Audio, was accepted. INTACT was put in touch with their local representative who was based at Edinburgh Castle, another Historic Scotland site which is already using ACT audio guides aimed at the general public.

INTACT arranged for a visit to Edinburgh Castle by a group of clients from an Edinburgh resource centre for adults with learning disabilities to see how practical they found these audio guides in use. The ACT guides are in the format of a CD player with earphones on a headband. The information is random access, the visitor keying in the number of the appropriate listening point which is identified with a headphone symbol. As well as the normal level of information, users can access more about topics they are particularly interested in by keying a further number.

The day centre group of four students and two members of staff were met by Shona McMillan, the Audio Tour Project Manager at the Castle, and her assistant. They gave everyone an audio guide and explained how to use the equipment. Most of the centre students were able to key in the numbers and understood how the system worked, though a few of them needed some help. However they all found the information provided by the script, even at the normal level, too long and too complex. Once they realised that they could switch off the guide when they had heard enough at a particular point and go on to the next, they enjoyed it more.

In spite of the very clear conclusions that the information on the Castle audio guide was too difficult for people with learning disabilities and that there was too much of it, everyone enjoyed the visit. The accompanying staff thought that the system had possibilities because of the increased choice and independence it gave the centre members.

Another visit to Jedburgh took place to look again at the site and possibilities. The aim was to tie any audio guide scripts to the information presented in words and in graphics on the existing boards at the viewpoints, photographs of which were taken for reference. We also looked in at the nearby Melrose Abbey which has taped guides. These are an older system which is not random access, so that the visitor is guided round the site and given the information in a pre-determined order. Parts of the script cannot be omitted, though it is possible to 'fast forward' the tape.

INTACT produced a draft script based on the existing information boards, the schools' workbook and a fairly recent publication about Jedburgh Abbey produced by Historic Scotland and written by Doreen Grove. After the experience of the day centre group at Edinburgh Castle, the information and language had to be kept simple. But we wanted it to include references to things people could relate to, such as how cold it would be in winter with no central heating, and things to notice or look out for such as the mason's marks on the stones in the abbey church.

INTACT are very grateful to Marion Fry and Doreen Grove from Historic Scotland who not only checked various versions of the draft script for historical accuracy and correct usage, but also came up with suggestions of their own. We acknowledge too the help from ACT in Edinburgh and London who also advised on the script and made sure that we had the right instructions to help people use the guides easily. As we wanted the equipment to be as easy to use as possible the format was to have information about the Visitor Centre displays immediately after the user instruction section, and then a section for each of the viewpoints, designated 1 to 7.

Finally, staff and centre members of Millside in Galashiels, which provides day services for adults with learning disabilities, helped us with comments on the language and content of the script.

The final script was recorded in a professional studio on digital tape and sent to London to have suitable music added.
It was then to be pressed on to compact discs with a view of the nave taken from the gallery above the west door printed on the front. This was taken by Shona McMillan of ACT and chosen to show this view to those with mobility problems who would be unable to see it for themselves.

The last minute stages had to be rushed because of project time constraints and because time was needed to trial the guide with invited groups of people with learning disabilities who would act as consultants. Shona and her technical manager installed a rack to charge and hold the guides, and ACT let us have a number of different types of headphones and single earpieces for visitors to try. This was to find out which type was easiest for people with learning disabilities to use, and to get round the problem, identified by some users at the Edinburgh Castle trial, that a full set of headphones cuts the user off from others in the group. This makes going round a site less of a social activity than it might be.

We also wanted to get feedback from ordinary visitors who would be invited to try the guide and comment on it. We are very grateful to the custodial staff at Jedburgh Abbey, particularly Mr Rowland Duncan, who helped with this.

A press launch was organised and a group of staff and centre users from Millside, who had helped with the script, were able to attend and give their first impressions.

The majority of comments were very favourable. A member of the press, who suggested that a guide in simple English for people with learning disabilities might be rather patronising, accepted that this was not the case when he tried it out himself. The Millside group varied greatly in ability, but all felt that the guides had added to the enjoyment of their visit. As the numbers on the information panels corresponded to the numbered messages on the guide, most people found this quite easy to use.

Other invited groups have since tested the audio guides and the response again has been mostly positive. They have included two of the three people who had visited from Duns earlier. The only adverse comments so far have been from one visitor with learning disabilities who found it 'boring' (but the accompanying carer reckoned that he was not interested in old buildings). Another was puzzled by the references to "canons", which he understood as "cannons" and was disappointed not to see any guns! We now realise that the one explanation given early in the script that the holy men who lived at Jedburgh Abbey were "canons" rather than "monks" was not enough and that this should have been repeated to avoid such a misunderstanding.

Most ordinary visitors who have tried the audio guide have found it useful. One made the suggestion that visitors could have been invited to stroll round the herb garden in the cloister.

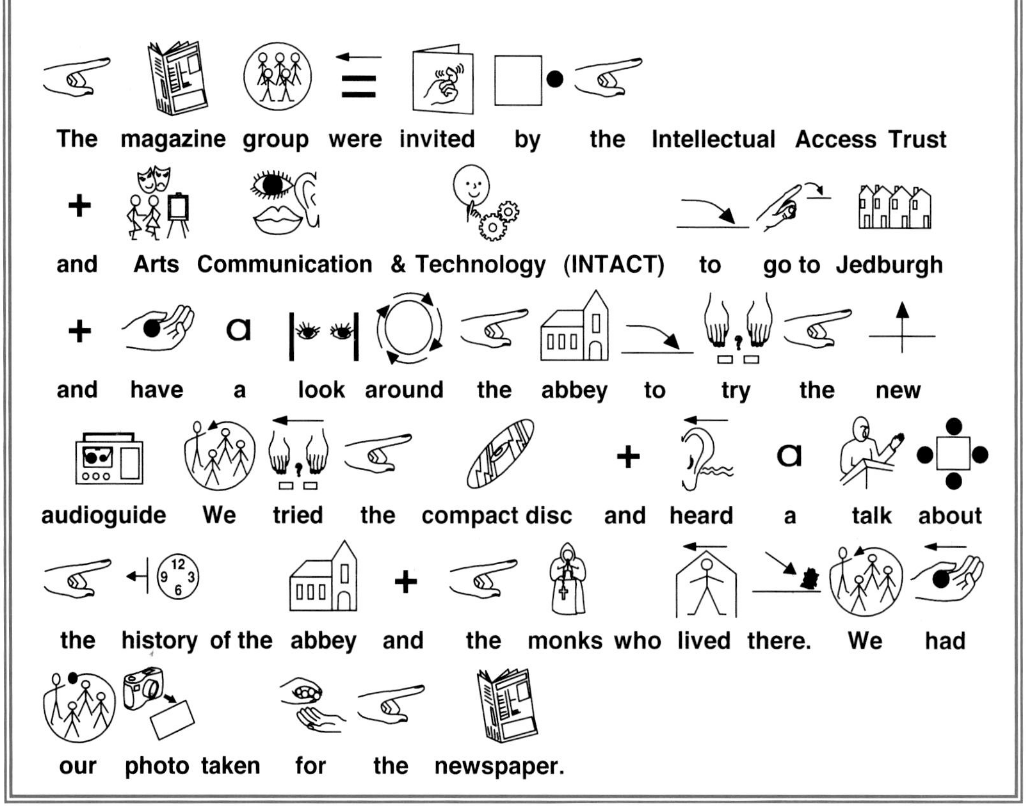
The magazine group were invited by the Intellectual Access Trust and Arts Communication & Technology (INTACT) to go to Jedburgh and have a look around the abbey to try the new audioguide We tried the compact disc and heard a talk about the history of the abbey and the monks who lived there. We had our photo taken for the newspaper.

Extract from Millside Magazine courtesy of Widgit Software

Visitors were usually quite happy with the conventional type of headphones which covered both ears, but the numbers were not enough for this to be significant. It is possible with this equipment for two people to share a guide with two sets of earphones plugged in so that they are hearing the information at the same time, but we have no reports from people actually doing this.

Unfortunately the trial happened while this report was being prepared. This has meant that because of pressure of time we have been unable to monitor it as closely as we would have liked.

How far were the aims achieved?

INTACT's aim in improving access to information about Jedburgh Abbey for people with learning and communication disabilities has been achieved through the use of audio guides.

We have learnt a great deal through this exercise which will be invaluable in producing a trial audio guide for the Museum of Scotland. These lessons include the need to work closely with appropriate experts and curators to ensure accuracy of information and the need for a clear script in straightforward English.

Historic Scotland's aims have also been met, including making them more familiar with the needs of people with learning or communication disabilities in general so that some of what is learnt at Jedburgh can be applied at other Historic Scotland sites. To help people with mobility problems who are unable to go round the site, INTACT has suggested that Historic Scotland might make copies of the information on the outside panels. These copies could be used in conjunction with the audio guide to give visitors more information about the parts of the abbey they can see from the Visitor Centre or from the viewing platform.

We feel too that ACT are more aware of the needs of people with learning disabilities and of the potential of audio guides for providing them with information in an accessible format. It was their staff who suggested that the equipment used in the Jedburgh trial should be modified so that the rewind button was yellow. This simplified the instructions to:

- **Green** – for start (after keying in the appropriate number)
- **Red** – for stop
- **Yellow** – for return to the beginning of the message

Their help at all stages has been invaluable and this experience of working together will be an advantage when we come to work on the script for a short, straightforward English audio guide to the Museum of Scotland. We are particularly grateful to Shona McMillan for her enthusiasm and commitment.

We recognised the need to have the script read by someone with exceptionally clear diction and the ability to vary pitch and speed of delivery. This was as important as the actual wording of the script and was achieved for us by Alasdair Hutton (the 'voice' of the Edinburgh Tattoo) and we are grateful to him.

By showing some of the wonderful objects in the Kelvingrove collection, it made the point that access is important just because these are things that everyone has the right to see and appreciate.

It is particularly important to look at ways of helping people with learning difficulties to share interests and to develop relationships, as well as to share access to and use of neighbourhood places.
Open University Workbook 2 for Course K668

This project is about the concerns people with learning disabilities have when visiting museums and galleries.

INTACT's Partners:

Museum staff at Kelvingrove Art Gallery and Museum, Glasgow

Tenants, support workers and Training Officer from Key Housing, Glasgow

Albavision, Inverness

Aims

Because of the different aims of the groups taking part, it was realised at the beginning that there would have to be a certain amount of compromise. Everyone should gain something from the scheme and feel 'ownership' of it.

Key Housing Tenants' Aims:

- to put across the tenants' concerns when visiting museums and galleries

- to show them as people with abilities who wish to be as independent as possible and have their own interests

Aims of Glasgow Museums' staff:

- to enable the Key Housing Tenants' Group, and others with similar disabilities, to access the displays and facilities within Glasgow Museums

- to find out about and, where possible, respond to the difficulties encountered by visitors with disabilities

INTACT's Aims:

- to help the Key Housing tenants to get across their concerns and to reconcile these with the Museums' desire to be shown in a positive light

- to have a final product which could be used for staff disability awareness training in museums and galleries

Consultation

A member of the Project's Steering Committee put INTACT in touch with Key Housing, which provides supported housing in the community for adults with a wide range of learning disabilities.

Their Training Officer invited INTACT to one of the Tenants' Meetings at the Glasgow Office. After a short explanation of what INTACT was about, the tenants were asked for their views. These reinforced other findings that people with learning disabilities often find museums frustrating places to visit as they are unable to get information about the objects or works of art on display because so much of it is in print. A number of people at this initial meeting particularly enjoyed visiting art galleries and taking part in art workshops.

Through these and other discussions, the idea of making a video emerged as a way in which the Tenants' Group could put across their point of view to museum professionals. Some of the tenants expressed interest in taking part. The idea was then put to Jem Fraser, Museum Education Officer for Glasgow Museums.

A meeting took place with three tenants, Emily, Robert and Malcolm. Crawford, who uses a wheelchair, was unable to be there but wanted to be part of the group. It was decided to look at access, how easy it is to find things, staff attitudes, how interesting the displays are and how easy it is to learn about them. Good points, such as it is a nice place to visit, is free and has a good café, were to be emphasised. A meeting at Kelvingrove Art Gallery and Museum was then arranged to identify which areas to film.

It was soon realised that for the video to have some impact and for it to be suitable for INTACT to use as a training aid, there would have to have some professional assistance, particularly with the editing. After a few approaches to various different organisations, help was offered at a very reasonable rate from Albavision, a studio based in Inverness. As the financial quotation included shooting as well as editing, it was gratefully accepted.

The Process

Making the Video

The preliminary visit to Glasgow's Kelvingrove Art Gallery and Museum had identified a temporary exhibition, *Claws*, which was on loan from the Hancock Museum in Newcastle. Everyone agreed that it would be useful to film the video while this was on display because of the subject matter (large and small cats) which appealed to the group, and the fact that there were a number of interactive displays in it which could be included as examples of the sort of exhibits which would help people with learning disabilities.

Albavision were able to take some preliminary background shots inside Kelvingrove, and then meet some of the tenants at the Key Housing office. The idea of this was to get to know them and to see some of their art work which they brought along to that meeting. For various reasons, including the absence of the Training Officer and the fact that lighting levels were not good, this did not achieve as much as had been hoped.

Public launch of *Get the Picture* by tenants of Key Housing

However a story board was planned after some discussion and Crawford drew some ideas on a big sheet of paper while the others present made suggestions as to what should be included. All agreed on the need to make important points about both physical and intellectual access but without being too emphatic. It was also decided that examples of good practice should be included.

Because *Claws* was soon to complete its run, the main filming had to be scheduled very quickly. The outside shots proved difficult as the date chosen turned out to be very wet. Unfortunately too, Robert could not come so we were down to three tenants for the main filming.

Like many buildings of its time, Kelvingrove Art Gallery and Museum has flights of steps to the main entrance. Since making the video, the museum has installed an adapted entrance for those with mobility problems just beside these steps. However, on the filming day, Crawford and his support worker had to go all the way to the back of the building in the rain to find a level entrance. They joined the rest of the group in the main hall after a slight delay.

Ceramic work by tenants of Key Housing

Within the *Claws* exhibition, Emily was filmed using an interactive computer by means of a tracker ball, Malcolm using lift-up labels concealing the answers to questions about animal markings, and both he and Crawford using the light-up display panel. There was an exhibit with both a cat's and a dog's paw which was intended to make the point, by direct comparison, that the cat's claws are retractable. The idea behind this display was good and the attempt to let people actually feel the difference was far more useful than any amount of words. It was unfortunate that the design of Crawford's wheelchair, combined with his difficulty in stretching, meant that he could not experience this for himself, though the others could, and understood the point being made.

Emily enjoyed demonstrating the museum's "Talking Mummy" in the main hall which is activated when a visitor makes a donation. Then the group went to the upper floor and looked at some of the art displayed there.

Everyone was intrigued by the actual process of filming and by the care taken to make sure the camera was level on the tripod and that the lighting was as good as it could be without having special equipment. It all took much longer than expected so everyone was glad to take a break in the café. Some shots were filmed there and the storyboard was checked to make sure we had included all we wanted.

The editing

A first rough version was put together and INTACT made some suggestions about incorporating material from the earlier shoot. Shots of the story board and of a sketch made by Emily, inspired by the "Talking Mummy" in the main hall, were to be included. Some details on the voice-over were to be changed, as well as a suggestion that Jem Fraser record the introduction on tape so that this could be dubbed in. Meantime, the Hancock Museum in Newcastle had been contacted to get their approval for filming inside *Claws*.

This improved version was put together and shown to the Museum Education Officer and the people from Key Housing who had taken part. Everyone was reasonably happy with it at this stage, though further modifications were suggested.

- Glasgow Museums requested that a statement about the planned improvements to the access for wheelchair users at Kelvingrove should be included

- INTACT and Key Housing both asked if it would be possible for the voices of the tenants to be dubbed on, in the same way that Jem Fraser's had been added. When the filming was taking place, the background noise often swamped the tenants' comments as they were not accustomed to projecting their voices. We hoped this would be a way to get more of their actual words on the video, as this would be better than relying on the narrator's voice-over to give their views

- The Key Housing Training Officer suggested that more might be made of the fact that all the tenants portrayed in the video not only enjoyed looking at art, but were themselves creative artists, working with groups like the Project Ability Centre for Developmental Arts

The statement about the improved access for wheelchair users was duly included along with Jem Fraser's introduction but the attempts made to record comments from the tenants were not very successful. Firstly, it was difficult to fix a recording session to do this because of their holiday arrangements and, when this was finally arranged, the recorded results were not very good so only one or two brief comments could be added.

However, some shots of art work done by tenants, with support from Project Ability, and which are displayed in the Key Housing Offices, were included on the video before we ran out of time.

Finishing Touches

A meeting was also arranged with the three tenants and Jem Fraser when they were able, along with some care staff, to put across directly some of their concerns about museum visiting. At one time we had thought of filming this meeting, but the logistics of getting everyone together were too difficult and we were told that filming a convincing looking discussion would require more than one camera and the participants would all have to be 'miked up' which was well beyond our budget.

The resulting draft version of the video was shown to the members of the INTACT Steering Committee, one of whom suggested putting captions on the tape for the benefit of anyone with a hearing impairment. After some discussion with Albavision, who were arranging for the copying of the master tape to be done, captions were put on one version.

Albavision were extremely helpful throughout the making of this video, in spite of the number of changes which were suggested at different stages. Not having been involved in such an exercise before, it was a revelation to see how much was involved in filming and editing even a relatively short video.

The same draft version was also shown at a MAGDA (Museums and Galleries Disability Association) seminar at the GEM (Group for Education in Museums) 1997 Conference in Cardiff. It was well received there; one delegate suggested that a copy should be sent to every museum director in the country.

Julian Spalding, Director of Glasgow Museums at the time, saw the video before the launch and gave his approval.

I think it is very helpful in showing and spelling out some of the straightforward problems that people with learning disabilities face when visiting museums, and how these can be overcome with a bit of thought and consideration. It is most positive because it is so honest and direct.

The launch of the final version took place in the Conference Room at Kelvingrove Art Gallery and Museum. The tenants all took part and their friends and families came, along with representatives from the

Museum, Key Housing and INTACT. For the purpose of the press release a title was needed and *Get the Picture* was approved. It was very appropriate that the captioned version was shown at this event, as one member of this audience was profoundly deaf.

Copies were given to the organisations who took part in this venture or were represented on the Steering Committee; Glasgow Museums and Galleries, Key Housing, Enable, Disability Scotland and the Scottish Museums Council.

Evaluation

As well as being shown in a draft version at the GEM/MAGDA Conference, the video has been shown to members of Disability Scotland's Leisure and Arts Committee, to delegates on a course for museum professionals run by the Scottish Centre for Cultural Management and Policy, and to a group of museum professionals, including a high proportion of curators, in Dundee. An Edinburgh Resource Centre for adults with learning disabilities borrowed it to show to their Members' Council.

The reactions from these showings to a variety of audiences have been very favourable. The video makes its points clearly but without over-emphasis on the negative side. The examples of good practice shown are effective and most viewers seemed to feel that the fact that the video is a compromise between different standpoints on museum access is actually a strength.

One trainer who borrowed it found the references to the problems of those with physical disabilities rather confusing. This came about because one of the tenants is a wheelchair user as well as having a communication disability.

By showing some of the wonderful objects in the Kelvingrove collection, it made the point that access is important just because these are things that everyone has the right to see and appreciate.

Were the Aims achieved?

Given the very different aims of the parties involved in making *Get the Picture*, a reasonable balance was achieved. The aims quoted at the start were all met and the lessons learnt in the actual process were very important. The different groups learnt a great deal about the needs of the others.

It was a pity that we were unable to record more of the actual voices of the tenants giving their reactions. Our attempt to insert more later was unsuccessful. However, the tenants' views were put across indirectly and they were fully consulted as to what was said on their behalf.

The video has already been shown to various groups who have responded to it positively as a way of raising awareness of the needs of people with learning disabilities when visiting museums and galleries.

Longer term effects

Following the useful meeting between the group of tenants and Glasgow Museums' Education Officer, we hope that this consultation will continue. An invitation was extended to the Key Housing Tenants' Group to look at some of the planned improvements at the People's Palace, reopening in April 1998, but this did not happen because of time constraints. However we hope that they will be consulted in the plans for Kelvingrove 2001 about the access needs of people with learning disabilities.

Key Housing intend to use their copy of *Get the Picture* as part of training for their care staff, and to show to their tenants' groups. As they operate in many parts of Scotland, this may encourage many more of their tenants who are living in the community, and the staff who support them, to think that museum visiting is a rewarding activity wherever they are.

Finally, we are glad to be able to report that the new accessible entrance to Kelvingrove Museum and Art Gallery opened in the spring of 1998. There is now a lift to the left of the steps to the main front entrance which takes wheelchair users and others with mobility problems to the level of the main hall. This was especially designed to fit the stonework of the front façade of this beautiful listed building.

Technology is not a substitute for the experience of seeing an object or a work of art, but can provide information which will enhance that experience.

... provided the information is presented in an accessible manner, people with learning difficulties often respond effectively to the interactive nature of computers[1]
The Informability Manual HMSO (1996)

INTACT wanted to explore the possibilities of using computers as a way of giving information about museum or gallery displays to people with learning disabilities. However, though we were interested in exploring the uses of computer technology, our knowledge of this area was slight, so we were dependent on advice from others. INTACT's contribution was to:

- assess whether people with learning disabilities liked computer interactives and found them easy to use
- identify some of the problems and look at possible solutions
- suggest additions to existing guidelines on computer interactives to help people with learning disabilities

INTACT's Partners:

National Museums of Scotland
Multimedia Team

Ceres Computer Consultants

Edinburgh International Science Festival

Capability Scotland

Scottish Council for Educational Technology

Communication Aids for Language and Learning, Edinburgh University

KEYCOMM, Edinburgh

Aims

- to find out what modifications needed to be made to an existing computer programme to make it easier to use for people with learning disabilities
- to assess the ease of use and learning potential of this modified programme
- to look at the use of existing computer interactives in museums and galleries, to assess their learning potential and suggest some recommendations to improve their suitability for people with learning disabilities
- to see what could be achieved by using specialised but commercially available products to give people with disabilities such as severe cerebral palsy the ability to access databases such as MOSAICS (Museum of Scotland Advanced Interactive Computer System)

There were three aspects to this project:

1. modifying an existing computer programme to make it more suitable for use by people with learning disabilities, assessing how effective these changes were and how effective the programme was as a learning technique

2. looking at the use of computer interactives in existing museum displays and assessing their suitability for people with learning and communication disabilities

3. giving access to a data base for people who had a good understanding of the kind of information they wanted but, because of communication or motor disabilities (for example people with cerebral palsy), were unable to do this by an ordinary keyboard, mouse or touch screen

Design your own Tartan

As a way of testing ideas on how computer programmes could be adapted for people with learning disabilities, an existing programme which had been developed by Dr Uist Macdonald of Ceres Computer Consultants Limited for the Royal Museum of Scotland Discovery Room, was considered.

This had been part of a Scottish theme and fitted in with books on the history of tartan, examples of various tartans and lengths of tartan cloth which visitors could use, following the simple instructions, to dress themselves in a belted kilt and plaid.

The original computer programme explained something of how tartan is woven and how the pattern is created before inviting visitors to design their own by choosing colours from a selection of bobbins on screen and arranging these as a warp. Once the choice of colours and relative amounts of each were chosen, the visitor pressed a key to "make your own tartan". The computer then proceeded to weave in the same colours for the weft. As this happened, the colours blended and the distinctive effect of a traditional tartan weave could be seen.

If the visitor was happy with the result, it could be printed off so that s/he could have a record of the design to keep. Understandably this was a popular attraction at the Discovery Room and the facilitators were often hard pressed to keep up with the demand.

Users with learning disabilities had experienced some problems with the original programme, so it was decided to consult SCET (Scottish Council for Educational Technology). They suggested some possible modifications. However, as the programme copyright was owned by Dr Macdonald, he was contacted and agreed to modify it.

With help from the Esmée Fairbairn Charitable Trust, INTACT purchased a suitable computer and printer. To make the programme more user friendly for people with learning disabilities Dr Macdonald made a number of modifications:

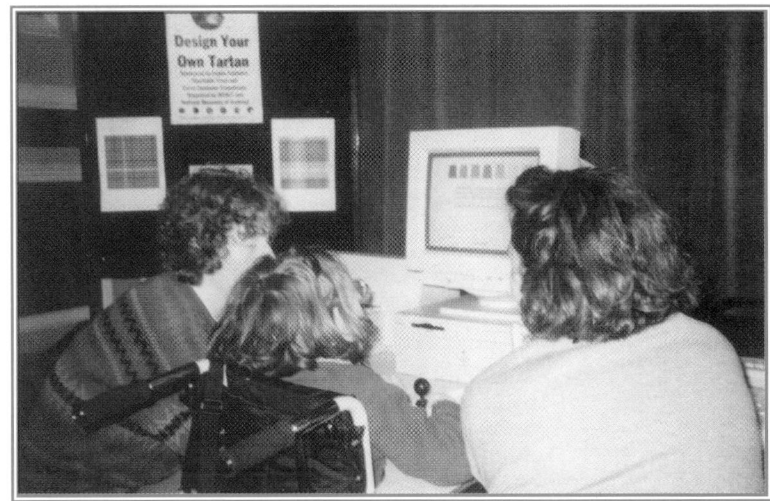

Design Your Own Tartan at Edinburgh International Science Festival

1. There was a lot of text on the screen in the original version, so this was cut down and voice prompts were added.

2. The first part of the programme was simplified and shortened. Terms like "warp" and "weft" were explained through the use of different colours. Animation was used to make the different ways of repeating the design easier to follow. (Unfortunately, "horizontal" and "vertical", referring to the warp and weft, were not changed to more easily understood terms).

3. A demonstration was given of how to choose colours from the bobbins, and more time was given for this choice, with a chance to try again if the person was not happy. This was because not everyone realised that the position of the pointer on the warp bar was crucial to how much of that colour was laid down.

It was interesting that there were no complaints that the programme was too easy or too slow, which bears out our conviction that what helps people with learning disabilities, helps the general public too.

4. Dr Macdonald also wrote a special programme for the computer to work directly on line with a specific printer so that people would not have to wait so long before receiving their print-out. This was a much cheaper option than buying an expensive super-fast printer.

Specialised Ke:nx switchgear had been purchased in the hope that the programme could be used by people who had restricted movement and could only operate a "one-touch" switch. However, it turned out to be far more complicated than had first been thought to make the programme scannable by such a device.

It was arranged to try out the equipment at the Assembly Rooms as part of the Edinburgh International Science Festival in April 1997 and it was advertised in their programme. Since the special switch gear was not appropriate for this programme, a Kensington 'Turbo-Mouse', a tracker ball with extra large programmable buttons for easy use, was purchased. This was to help those who found the conventional mouse difficult. It was possible for users to choose whether they preferred this device or the conventional mouse by wiring them in parallel.

Edinburgh International Science Festival Trial Findings

The *Design Your Own Tartan* computer programme was advertised as part of EISF in 1997, but for the first week only.

Though this had been flagged up as 'user friendly' and particularly suitable for people with learning disabilities, the majority of those who came were members of the general public, many of them families with children. It was interesting that there were no complaints that the programme was too easy or too slow, which bears out our conviction that what helps people with learning disabilities, helps the general public too.

A number of groups of people with learning disabilities from day centres came, some pre-booked and some while visiting other events at the Festival. Most people were well able physically to cope with the equipment, particularly if they used the Turbo-Mouse, and most grasped the idea of what they had to do to design their tartan.

It was sad to see how difficult a small number of people found it to make a choice of the available colours for themselves. Some asked accompanying members of staff what they should pick, and one woman just took the colours in the order they were presented on the bobbins. This showed that making choices for themselves is still an unfamiliar and frightening idea for some people with learning disabilities and how far many of them still are from being able to choose things like leisure activities.

As most schools in the area were on their Easter break at the time of the Festival, only a few groups of school pupils attended. However one group which did included a boy with severe dyslexia and he was able to use the programme without too much difficulty because much of the information was provided graphically. Unfortunately, the benefit from the voice prompts was diminished by the unavoidably high noise level at the Festival venue.

We also had several young people with cerebral palsy who came with family members. Some could use the Turbo-Mouse, but one girl (who attends a mainstream primary school) had such severe problems that she managed only with great difficulty. However she was absolutely determined to succeed and was overjoyed when her own design eventually came out of the printer. One of the INTACT Trustees who was in attendance said that her smile made the whole project worthwhile.

By asking people about what they understood from the programme, something of how much people with learning disabilities could learn from it could be determined. Not surprisingly, this depended a great deal on the ability of the person, but many users volunteered the information that they understood more about the weaving process. Certainly a number of people remarked on the effect of the colours blending as the 'weaving' took place on the screen.

While it was not possible to measure the amount of extra information gained by users, it seemed that the majority, even among those with quite severe learning disabilities, did learn something. In many cases the use of the computer could be seen to encourage increased attention span, opportunities for making choices and social interaction in a group. What was in no doubt was that users enjoyed the experience of designing their own tartan and getting a personal print out of their own design. There also seemed to be some improvement in motor skills.

This may seem a very modest success. But for people who have limited opportunities for such activities, it was real progress.

Problems

There were a number of problems with the equipment which came to light as a result of the fairly intensive use it had during this trial. Many of these were connected with the printer which was a particularly sensitive piece of equipment. It had a tendency to crash if, for example, it was allowed to run out of paper, or another person started to use the programme too soon while it was still working on the previous design, or if the cursor went over the "return to start" button as a user was trying to give the "print" command.

It was also frustrating that it was not possible to skip the first, explanatory, part of the programme if there was a group using the computer. If those standing round watching had already seen this, they wanted to get on with doing their own design instead of going through the first part again.

Dr Macdonald was consulted after the trial about these difficulties. He was able to tell us how to skip parts of the programme as this facility was already built in (though we had not realised this), and made it less likely for the programme to crash before printing by making the "return to start" button less sensitive. The other problems with the printer were a matter of making sure that nothing was done to upset it!

Further Trials

The computer equipment was loaned to Capability Scotland centres at Upper Springland, Perth and Ellersly in Edinburgh, and their Westerlea School. As these were all facilities for people with cerebral palsy, there were some problems with the physical use of the equipment, but participants enjoyed using it and were pleased with the printed designs. Westerlea School was able to make a colourful wall display by laminating pupils' designs.

The computer was also used alongside the original version when the Discovery Room was open at the Royal Museum and, on its own, when it went to Callendar House, Falkirk. Again it was used mainly by school groups and the general public with no comments that the programme was too simple. At both venues there were visits by

the learner should always have control over what is being learned. Visitors should be able to investigate material how they want to, not how we want them to.

special school pupils and some groups of adults from day centres, which reinforced our previous findings.

Suitability of Computer Interactives for People with Learning or Communication Disabilities

Technology versus 'real' experience
This is not a real dilemma; what is important is that the technology is not a substitute for the experience of seeing an object (still less being able to handle it) or a work of art, but can provide information which will enhance that experience.

The main advantage of computer technology for people with learning disabilities, and for the general public as well, is the fact that it is, or should be, a flexible method of obtaining information with the user in control. It should encourage freedom of choice and 'browsing' behaviour, so the information should be presented in an accessible and attractive manner.

This independence in acquiring information is very important to people with learning disabilities. It gives them control and choice over the subject and amount of information they require. Computer interactives can incorporate a variety of media within their systems; sound, video, graphics and animation as well as text, so can be well suited to people who have difficulty in reading. They can provide links and references from one area of interest to another, they can enable the user to look at an enlarged detail of a picture or an object, or to see it in the round and view the side, back or even the base, and they can show more than one image on the screen at the same time so that they can be compared.

In an article in *Curator*[2] Beverly Serrell and Britt Raphling give ten practical design principles for using computers in exhibitions. An important one for people with learning disabilities is the sixth, where they say:

the learner should always have control over what is being learned. Visitors should be able to investigate material how **they** want to, not how **we** want them to.

In the same article they point out that computer text should use the same principles of language as any good interpretive label. These are that it should be short, clear and concise and fulfil legibility guidelines.

Unfortunately, computer interactives are very expensive in terms of both time and money, can usually be used by just one person at a time (though a slave screen can be watched by other people), and, inevitably, they go wrong. When this happens, it is both time-consuming and expensive to put them right again.

Interactive Computers in Museums

The research fell into two parts. The first was direct observation of people with learning or communication disabilities when the opportunity arose or where a group had been invited for that purpose. The second was the assessment of the suitability of examples of computer interactives in museums, based on experience of what worked and what did not.

Examples of the first group were from the Royal Museum of Scotland's *Art and Industry*, the Scottish Natural Heritage *Dolphin Watch* programme at Inverness and *Claws*, the Hancock Museum, Newcastle's travelling exhibition (when at Kelvingrove, Glasgow).

A group of students from Capability Scotland's Ellersly Centre for young adults with cerebral palsy were very critical of the access to the computer interactives in *Art and Industry*. As wheelchair users with limited upper body flexibility, they were unable to reach touch screens which were fixed into a vertical wall either between or alongside display cases.

The *Dolphin Watch* programme at Inverness gave some problems to a group from a local day centre who tried it. They found it difficult to get started as the visitor had to touch a leaping dolphin twice in quick succession which took some dexterity. Though there were some good graphics, there was a lot of text on the screen at times which the learning-disabled group found off-putting. Also having to stand while using it was tiring for everyone.

The computer interactives at *Claws*, using a commercial programme, which were at Glasgow's Kelvingrove Museum and Art Gallery when we filmed the video (referred to in a separate pilot project), were very easy to use. There was a seat for the user, a centrally placed tracker ball, a slave screen above, and the programme used easily understood symbols, such as a loudspeaker to indicate how to get sound, and a film-camera to indicate there was a moving, rather than a still, picture.

In the second group there were more examples. These included: Verdant Works, Dundee; *Animal Magic* at the City Art Centre, Edinburgh; a very wide range at the Cité of Science and Industry, la Villette, Paris; the *Earth Gallery* at the Science Museum, London; the *Microgallery* at the National Gallery, London; Buckinghamshire County Museum, Aylesbury; and *Lifetimes* at Croydon Clocktower.

There is no need to repeat existing guidelines for the use of computer interactives in museums and galleries (see next page), but comments can be offered on access specifically for those with learning disabilities. However, it should be noted that some of the existing guidelines on physical access to computer stations for wheelchair users need to be used with care.

Some of the recommended dimensions for knee/footplate space are not adequate for all situations, and the specifications on arm reach are not appropriate for people with limited upper body movement. If computer screens are installed at a height where people have to stand, they get quickly tired, and such arrangements are rarely appropriate for wheelchair users, especially if there is insufficient knee/footplate space.

Guidelines for use by people with learning disabilities

1. The obvious need, as recognised by the Smithsonian Institution's Guidelines for *Accessible Exhibition Design*[3] is for **simple instructions**, preferably presented through symbols or audio instead of, or in addition to, text. This is important both for the initial instructions on how to start the programme (there are few things more frustrating than being unable even to start), and the continuing ones about how to move around within it, including how to get back to the menu.

2. As many people with learning disabilities may not have good hand control, a tracker ball or touch screen is better than a mouse. If a tracker ball is to be used, it is easier for a left-handed person if it is positioned centrally. A higher percentage of people with learning disabilities are left-handed than is the case with the general population (20% as compared with 10% or so, depending on how you define handedness).

3. A touch screen should have fairly large sensitive areas to help people with poor hand control and allow for different angles from which it might be touched, depending on whether users are seated or standing, or variations in height.

4. A lot of text on the screen is off-putting for people with learning disabilities. Clear symbols or voice prompts are much more user friendly.

5. People also need time to react, particularly if they have to make a decision.

6. The same recommendations on legibility apply to computers as to other ways of conveying information. These are to use text sparingly, and to provide audio, video, animation and graphics as appropriate.

General guidelines or suggestions for the use of computer interactives in museums and galleries may be found in:

The Smithsonian Institution's Guidelines for ***Accessible Exhibition Design*** Washington (1996) especially pages 31 – 40

Museum Practice 5 (1997) Page 24

Interpretation (August 1996)

Computers on the Exhibit Floor Beverly Serrell and Britt Raphling first published in ***Curator*** 35 (3) (1992) and reprinted in ***Developing Museum Exhibitions for Lifelong Learning*** GEM/Stationery Office (1996)

Access to databases such as MOSAICS

As mentioned in the section on Interpretation, the Museum of Scotland will provide for visitors with a special interest an area housing several computer terminals linked to the Museum of Scotland Advanced Interactive Computer System (MOSAICS) and offering access to CD Roms giving more information about the displays. This will enable visitors to use the computerised database to get more information about the objects on show in the museum than could be presented as display text or labels.

In the longer term, visitors to museums, galleries and libraries throughout Scotland will also be able to get access to the Scottish Cultural Resources Access Network (SCRAN). This is the only information technology project so far to have been supported by the Millennium Commission and will consist of a database containing 1.5 million records of approximately 6 million items from Scotland's cultural heritage. They will have been drawn from museums, galleries, historic sites, libraries and monument records.

As the project develops, about 100,000 digitised images of important Scottish artefacts will be drawn from the database and linked to text and, in some cases, sound and film. This multimedia resource will be wholly interactive, giving access to Scotland's rich cultural heritage to all, whether they live in Lerwick or Lochmaben.

The SCRAN project – a partnership of the Scottish Museums Council, the National Museums of Scotland and the Royal Commission on the Ancient and Historical Monuments of Scotland – will encourage schools, colleges, libraries, museums and community centres to set up access points for teachers, curators, students, researchers and members of the public.

Normal access will be by conventional keyboard, mouse and screen display. This requires good vision, hand/eye co-ordination and fine hand control, so is not suited to the needs of visitors who have cerebral palsy or other conditions which impair control of small, exact hand movements. To give these visitors equal access is not simply a question of social justice, but a statutory duty in terms of the Disability Discrimination Act. This Act makes it unlawful to discriminate on the grounds of a person's disability in the provision of goods, facilities and services. Discrimination includes providing a lower standard of service, and disability is defined as including intellectual as well as physical and sensory impairment.

Accordingly, places providing access to computerised databases will have to cater for the needs of people who have difficulty in using a conventional keyboard or mouse. There are various designs of Tracker Ball which can be used as an alternative to a mouse and many museums already provide such a device, rather than touch screen access, where it is appropriate. The advantages over a mouse, apart from the size which makes it easier to control, is that it is fixed to the display, usually in a central position in relation to the screen. As a security measure, models where the ball cannot be removed from the socket are recommended. Joysticks are another possibility, though they may be more fragile than a tracker ball.

Modern computers already have facilities built into their operating systems which can alter the workings of the keyboard and mouse. Full details of these are available from the CALL Centre (Communication Aids for Language and Learning) at the University of Edinburgh, but briefly it is possible:

1. to change the speed of operation of the keyboard, for example to avoid repetition of letters when a key is held down too long. This helps users with a hand tremor or who have difficulty in coming off keys

2. to adjust the double click speed, for people who cannot double click quickly enough

3. to use the 'sticky key' facility. This helps people who are one-handed or have poor control in one hand and therefore have difficulty in holding down two or three keys at one time

4. to use 'mouse keys'. Instead of using the mouse to move the pointer on the screen, the arrow keys on the numeric pad on the right hand side of the keyboard can be used to move the pointer, select letters or words and to 'drag' – all the normal actions of a mouse

5. to use 'slow keys'. This helps to prevent accidental keystrokes by tremor of hand or finger

6. to reduce the speed of the mouse so that small accidental movements have less effect.

All these facilities can be accessed without extra cost on most modern computers.

It is possible to purchase keyguards, frames with holes fitting over the keyboard, which help guide the fingers on to particular keys. They are useful for people with hand tremor as they can rest their hands on the frame while locating the correct key.

'Expanded Keyboards' exist which are useful for people with poor fine hand control as they give bigger keys with more space between them. Conversely, miniature keyboards can be suitable for people with a small range of movement because, for example, of muscular dystrophy. Information about these is contained in *Alternatives to the Standard Keyboard*, CALL Centre Information Sheet 2.[4]

Modern computers already have facilities built into their operating systems which can alter the workings of the keyboard and mouse.

There are other more specialised devices for people with very limited movement who need a single touch switch. For this to work, a special interface has to be used which provides both the hard- and software needed to tell the computer how to understand single switch devices (which can be hand, chin, head or knee operated).

There are many different kinds of communication and motor problems associated with a condition such as cerebral palsy or stroke and it would be unreasonable for museums to provide for every variation. However, with a combination of the facilities already built into most modern computers, alternatives to the standard keyboard or a powerful device such as the Ke:nx interface which enables single touch switches or an alternative keyboard to be connected, it should be possible to cater for many people who might otherwise be denied access to computer-based information. It should be noted that most people who require specialised computer access may well have their own alternative keyboard or switch gear which they could bring with them and which could then be connected if the necessary interface were available.

INTACT has given a Ke:nx specialised interface, which we had already purchased, to the Museum of Scotland Multimedia Team. With help from a KEYCOMM Development Officer (see Notes) who worked with multimedia staff, we hope that this equipment can be used in one of the computers for public access with the necessary set-ups to make programmes scannable. This should make access to the MOSAICS database and Museum of Scotland CD-Roms available to people with a variety of motor problems who require single switch access. As well as Ke:nx, INTACT has also passed on a number of such single touch switches, and we are assured that anyone requiring a very specific type of switch adapted to their individual needs would be able to plug such a device into a Ke:nx port and thus gain access to the programme.

Although it is unlikely that we will be able to test the full capabilities of this equipment before the end of the full-time INTACT Project, it is undoubtedly powerful and flexible and should enable people with a variety of disabilities, particularly those resulting from cerebral palsy, to obtain additional information about museum objects and to access the MOSAICS database.

How far were the aims achieved?

1. The findings about the sort of modifications needed to make a computer programme suitable for use by people with learning disabilities are incorporated in the guidelines given earlier and reflect much of what we have said about making other forms of information accessible. Our research suggests that such modifications make computers easier to use for most visitors, without detracting from the enjoyment of those who are fully able and computer literate.

2. The research showed that computer interactives are generally liked by people with learning disabilities because of the elements of choice and control they give.

3. A fair amount of information has been collected about ways of providing access to a computer database by people with cerebral palsy and similar conditions, but we have been unable to assess the use of the specialised equipment in practice.

However, it is necessary to add a warning. As our experience with the *Design Your*

Own Tartan computer programme showed us, computers are not cheap and they do have a tendency to break down, especially if they are heavily used by a large number of users, not all of whom are computer literate. Even a relatively small problem, such as the broken connection which we suffered, can put a machine out of action for some time if there is no back-up support immediately available. A computer which does not work irritates visitors and gives them a negative impression.

Note

As the area of special access technology is multi-disciplinary, it may be necessary to contact a number of services, (education, health etc) to get the necessary information on equipment and expertise.

National Centres and Services

Scotland

CALL (Communication Aids for Language and Learning) Centre • 4 Buccleuch Place • Edinburgh EH8 9LW • Tel 0131 667 1438 • Fax 0131 668 4220

KEYCOMM • St Giles Centre • 40 Broomhouse Crescent • Edinburgh EH11 3UB • Tel 0131 443 6775

MicroCentre Applied Computer Studies Division • University of Dundee • Dundee DD1 4HN • Tel 01382 23181 • Fax 01382 23435

SCET (Scottish Council for Educational Technology) • 74 Victoria Crescent Road • Glasgow G12 9JN • Tel 0141 337 5000 • Fax 0141 337 5050

SCTCI (Scottish Centre of Technology for the Communication Impaired) • Victoria Infirmary NHS Trust • Rutherglen Maternity Hospital • 120 Stonelaw Road • Rutherglen • Glasgow • G73 2PG • Tel 0141 201 6426/26 • Fax 0141 201 6423

England

ACE Centre • Ormerod School • Wayneflete Road • Headington • Oxford OX3 8DD • Tel 01865 63508 • Fax 01865 750188

NCET (National Council for Educational Technology) Milburn Hill Road • Science Park • Coventry CV4 7JJ • Tel 01203 416994 • Fax 01203 411418

The Computability Centre • PO Box 94 • Warwick • Warwickshire • CV34 5WS • Tel 01926 312847 • Fax 01926 311345

Wales

Communication Aids Centre • Rookwood Hospital • Fairwater Road • Llandaff Road • Cardiff CF5 2YN • Tel 01222 566281

Northern Ireland

Communication Aids Centre • Musgrave Park Hospital • Stockman's Lane • Belfast BT9 7JB • Tel 01232 669501

Ke:nx can be obtained from:
Don Johnston Special Needs • 18 Clarendon Court • Calver Road • Winwick Quay • Warrington • WA2 8QP • Tel 01925 241642

References

1. *The Informability Manual* W Gregory **HMSO** (1996)

2. *Computers on the Exhibition Floor* B Serrell and B Raphling *Curator* 35 (3) (1992)

3. *Accessible Exhibition Design* J Majewski **Smithsonian Institution** Washington (1997)

4. *Alternatives to the Standard Keyboard* CALL Information Sheet 2 **CALL Centre** Edinburgh University

Coming soon:

Special access technology P Nisbet and P Poon **CALL Centre** Edinburgh (1998). This will give full details of what is available, what it does and a list of suppliers.

Handling Sessions – Edinburgh

Physical involvement is a necessary condition for learning for children, and highly desirable for adults in many situations, but it is not sufficient. All hands-on activities must also pass the test of being minds-on — they must provide something to think about as well as something to touch. George Hein[1]

This project arose from the many comments we received that one thing visitors with learning disabilities would very much like to do at a museum is to be able to handle real objects.

INTACT'S partners:

National Museums of Scotland (NMS) Schools Officer

Staff and students from local adult day centres and further education college special needs departments

Aim

The aim was very simple: to allow groups of students from day centres and college special needs departments access to the handling collections in the Royal Museum, which is part of NMS, in response to a need that had already been expressed.

The Process

At the Royal Museum there was already a regular programme of handling training sessions for teachers who came from primary, secondary and special schools. They were run by the Schools Officer so that teachers who had attended would then be able to bring groups of pupils into the museum to work with the objects, either in the Education Centre or in an appropriate gallery.

There are four themed collections of objects:

- Ancient Egypt
- Plains Indians
- The Victorians, which included items of clothing as well as household objects
- On Planet Earth (rocks, minerals, fossils and rubber moulds for plaster casts)

The sessions are popular and well attended. The subsequent visits by pupils bring a whole new dimension to education in the museum and provide a unique and enjoyable experience. INTACT was keen to let people with learning disabilities share this kind of experience.

As teachers from special schools already attended the Handling Training Sessions, INTACT was able to negotiate with the Schools Officer to make them available also to day centre and college staff. They too would then be able to bring groups of their students to use the objects in the handling collections.

Letters were sent to day centre and college staff inviting them to apply for places on the next four sessions (corresponding to the four collections) which were held at the Royal Museum from 4.30 to 6.00 or 6.30pm. It was explained that, while the training was designed primarily for school teachers, college and day centre staff would find many suggestions for ways in which they could use the sets of objects with adults with learning disabilities.

Three members of staff (two from day centres and one from a college) came to the first set of four sessions, and the immediate feedback was positive. Those who attended appreciated that the sessions were designed for school teachers and that they were very much in the minority, although they were made welcome, made to feel part of the group and were able to ask questions specific to their needs as staff working with adults with learning disabilities.

They generally felt that they would need time to plan visits with their groups, and some set aside time to look again at the relevant galleries in the museum in order to do this.

Further sessions were run at which the numbers varied from one to five for each group of sessions. This proportion did not increase even for the December '97 sessions when special education teachers and day centre/college staff working with people with disabilities were especially targeted.

Results

At first this slow take-up seemed disappointing, particularly as these training sessions had been opened to day centre and college staff in response to a need that they themselves had identified. However, the staff concerned assured us that the problem was not lack of interest, but of time and resources. Effectively they, like teaching staff, were having to give up their own time to attend these sessions out of hours and, having already done a full day's work beforehand, this was not always possible. One person, who was initially very keen, was promoted within his organisation, with the result that he was no longer able to take groups out because of the management workload.

The same considerations applied to staff bringing groups of students once they had been trained. Both day centres and college special needs departments have tight budgets for staff and resources. They also have a structured day which can make it complicated to withdraw students from their regular timetable and are dependent on having enough staff and transport available before a group can go out.

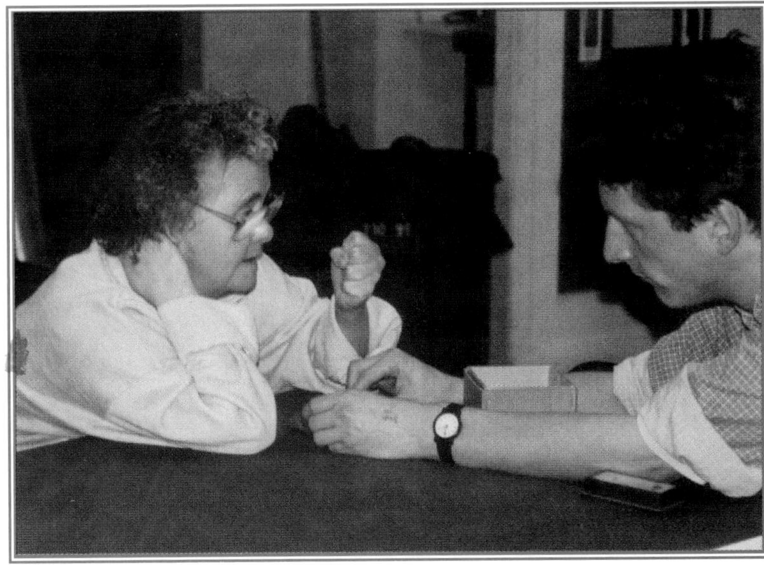

Geology Handling Session in Royal Museum, Edinburgh

One extremely keen day centre officer came to a whole set of four sessions and he was the first to bring a group of students to do handling with the Victorian objects.

From notes recorded at the time:

A group of eight adults with a variety of learning disabilities came to a handling session with the Victorian objects in the Education Centre. This was mainly successful though some of the group appeared not to be very involved. Most seemed to enjoy it on the whole and a few were very keen. It was certainly better than just wandering round looking at things, but many of them did not have much idea as to what the objects were, and were fairly passive, handing them on to someone who was more vocal or just saying *"I don't know"* when asked what they thought something was or what it was made of.

Knowing the collection enabled me to manage such diversity so that everyone could benefit from the visit. Although prepared, I was surprised at how quickly time vanished.

They all liked the parasol, the ostrich feather fan and the toasting fork and responded to these.

It was an advantage being in the Education Centre so that they could concentrate on the objects rather than being distracted by other people. Some of the group were reluctant to handle objects at first but later became interested. One man seemed indifferent and would not touch anything, yet made one or two sensible suggestions when the others were puzzled. The group just managed to get through all the objects in the time available, but did not try the clothing. They got tired quickly, not having a very long attention span, and needed a tea break part-way through.

Another group came to do a later session, but were unable to use the Education Centre as it was then occupied by the "Discovery Room". Because of this, they could not make plaster casts of fossils (an option with the geology materials), but they were very impressed with some of the large rocks which could be touched in the Geology Gallery and with the splendid display there of minerals and crystals.

It was not possible to monitor another Victorian handling session with a group of college students because of other commitments, but we were sent useful feedback from the college tutor.

We greatly enjoyed our visit to the museum although our arrival was delayed slightly due to difficulties in finding suitable parking for the mini-bus. Time was one of the most significant features of the visit, that and pre-visit preparation. I was very glad I'd attended the training session for staff, knowing what was available enabled me to prepare the students beforehand.

This paid dividends on the day of the visit as we could immediately focus on our interests. Some students were keen to look at costumes, others at artefacts and there were those who had a general interest and wanted to look at everything. Knowing the collection enabled me to manage such diversity so that everyone could benefit from the visit. Although prepared, I was surprised at how quickly time vanished. I will in future allow 1 hour for intense study of objects. I think this is the limit of the students' attention span. Then a half hour each end for arrival, introduction, organisation and tidy up.

One very popular activity was trying on clothes and having photographs taken. I wonder if it would be possible to develop this more? Perhaps if funding allowed, a more extensive wardrobe, even reproduction costumes would work. This 'dressing up' aspect really helped students appreciate the 'hidden' nature of Victorian life. My graphic description of corsets would have been greatly enhanced by a demonstration of the restricting nature of tight laces. A video demonstrating objects in use would also be wonderful, if funds were available.

Thank you and colleagues in the museum for helping to make our visit so enjoyable.

Subsequently a small group of four students came with a day centre officer to use the geology handling objects in the Education Centre of the museum and this group was monitored by INTACT.

Again the student involvement varied a lot but the member of staff, who knew the group well, was able to include everyone in the discussions and encourage them to look at particular aspects such as the weight of the object, the feel, the shape or the colour. He was able to create an atmosphere where the students were able to speculate about the objects without any fear of being put down, while being gently steered towards something close to the right answer by suggesting ideas they were familiar with. Everyone enjoyed the fossil-casting and was successful in making a cast to take away.

How far was the aim fulfilled?

As groups of students from day centres and college special needs departments were able to have access to the Royal Museum handling collections, we were successful.

However the response was not as great as we had hoped mainly because of the problems staff face in finding time to attend the training sessions, fitting handling visits into centre or college timetables, or having the staff and transport available to take groups out.

What lessons were learned?

It is necessary to have someone doing the handling training who can respond to the needs of a variety of trainees: teachers (primary, secondary, or special school), college tutors or day centre staff. They will all have their own background experience and their own agenda for the groups they wish to bring to the museum after training. We were lucky in the Schools Officer at NMS to have someone who did respond to these differing needs.

It is useful to have an area, such as the Royal Museum Education Centre, where students with learning disabilities can handle objects without too many other distractions going on. For most of them, this is a new experience and they need time to adjust to it and to the level of concentration required.

The member of staff doing the handling session does not need to be an expert in the material being used. As well as the training, notes are provided by the museum. However he or she does have to plan ahead and be able to adapt their use to the capacities of the members of the group. This knowledge, plus his/her own expertise in helping them to relate museum objects to what they know already and encouraging interaction within the group are the most important qualities.

If museum staff are already doing handling training sessions, making these available for day centre and college staff, or other community groups, is not a great additional expense. Although the take-up for handling sessions has been slow initially, INTACT hopes that the use will increase and that the Royal Museum handling collections will be a valuable resource for people with learning disabilities.

There are other less formal ways in which museum visitors can have access to things to touch. A number of museums already do this: sometimes in the form of a collection which can be borrowed by schools or community groups, sometimes in an education or discovery area and sometimes in a gallery alongside cased objects. All of these are extremely valuable and are appreciated by those who use such facilities. Which way is chosen will depend on the museum concerned, the particular collection and factors such as space and resources.

However, useful though such ways of providing handling experience are, INTACT believes that the opportunity for the staff who know the students to be able to work with them is particularly valuable for those with learning disabilities. To have time to look carefully, to be free from distractions, to turn objects around in one's hands and, above all, to speculate and discuss findings with others, make the sessions at the Royal Museum especially appropriate for people with learning disabilities.

It is certainly worth emphasising that it is not only children and school groups who appreciate the chance to handle objects. This has already been mentioned in the section on learning in museums where the need for a multi-sensory approach is stressed for adults and children alike. A museum could provide a selection of handling objects in appropriate areas, perhaps with labels in large print, Makaton symbols, Braille or in audio form alongside the conventional ones. By making some objects available for everyone to handle and providing information in easily accessible formats they would be demonstrating a commitment to the idea of an inclusive service.

Reference

1. G Hein, *Proceedings of ICOM/CECA Conference* (1991)

The Disability Policy should incorporate a procedure for regular consultation with disabled people and disability organisations, in order to assist in designing, improving and developing the provision of services and the recruitment and employment of disabled people.
Museums and Galleries Commission *Guidelines on Disability for Museums and Galleries in the United Kingdom* (1992)

Highlands and Islands Enterprise had agreed to help fund the work of INTACT on the understanding that at least one of the pilot projects was located in the Highlands. This accorded with our own wish to show that our work was just as relevant in areas outside the central belt of Scotland. Inverness was an obvious choice, as the town has a great many visitors and good communications to a wide catchment area with a range of community activities.

We contacted Catharine Niven, Curator of Inverness Museum and Art Gallery which includes an art gallery as well as displays about local geology, natural history, archaeology and social history. It has a lively programme of changing exhibitions which has featured the work of Scottish and international artists and photographers, as well as the work of local crafts groups. There are already a number of objects in the open displays which can be touched; stones in the geology area and some specimens in the natural history section. The worn areas on the latter demonstrate very clearly why not all the animals can be touched.

Temporary displays feature the work of community groups or voluntary organisations such as the Association for the Protection of Rural Scotland or they may be on themes with a local relevance such as the experience of evacuees during the First World War. There are talks by museum curators and others and there is a loan service for school and community groups. Unfortunately, the access for wheelchair users is limited. There is a ramp to the front door and a stair lift to the first floor, so that the display areas, shop and café are accessible, but the toilets in the basement are not.

INTACT's partners:

Staff at Inverness Museum and Art Gallery

Staff and members of the Corbett Resource Centre

Staff and trainees of the SHIRLIE Project (SHIRLIE stands for: Support, Help, Initiative, Recreation, Leisure, Independence and Education)

Staff and students from Cantraybridge College of Rural Studies

Aims of the Project

Inverness Museum and Art Gallery:

The Curator said the museum already had frequent visits from parties of people with learning and communication disabilities. Her aims in working with INTACT were:

- to do this in a slightly more formal way
- to learn more about the particular needs of this group of visitors
- to glean ideas for a planned discovery area within the museum

INTACT's aims were:

- to encourage contacts between the museum and local organisations for people with learning disabilities in order to fulfil

Museums tend to put too much reliance on written text, the writing is often too small and too many big words are used

the first two museum aims

- to include people with learning disabilities in the consultation process for setting up the discovery area

The Process

INTACT contacted a number of local organisations concerned with learning disabilities and were able to set up two meetings in Inverness.

The first was arranged with help from the manager of the Corbett Resource Centre, who provided the venue, and included some of its own staff and centre members, staff and trainees from the SHIRLIE Project, a deputy head teacher from the local special school, and a representative from Cantray-bridge College which teaches rural skills to young adults with learning disabilities.

In a lively meeting the following main points were made:

- museums tend to put too much reliance on written text, the writing is often too small and too many big words are used

- the use of audio guides, video, computers and the availability of things to touch and do, would help those with learning disabilities to understand more about the displays. The rocks and stuffed animals which could be touched were liked

- the use of symbols and pictures on signs, on instructions for interactives, and on publicity leaflets and materials would be helpful

Other points were that the group liked frequent changes in the displays, suggesting material could be taken from store in rotation, and that it was not always easy to find out what was on. They welcomed the museum's outreach efforts, but would like more.

A meeting at the museum to discuss ideas for the discovery area was attended by Catharine Niven, curators in Archaeology, Natural Science and Social History, an architect and a representative from Ross and Cromarty Cultural and Leisure Services.

The proposed development was to move the present museum shop to the foyer to make room for the new discovery area. This was to be a flexible multi-purpose resource which could be used as a self-service study/information centre, a class-room for educational/special interest groups or a small lecture room. It could include a computer link to SCRAN (Scottish Cultural Resources Access Network), 'hands-on' real objects plus microscopes and large hand lenses, local history records and both computerised and lo-tech interactives. There might be a satellite dish giving real time weather reports. It would be bookable by schools and other education groups but otherwise would be open to the public.

A number of other lo-tech interactives were planned for other areas of the museum such as the Railway and Natural History displays so that the investigative spirit and style of the centre should carry through to the main displays. Consultation with likely user-groups was discussed and, as a result, a meeting between museum curators and some of the people who had attended the Corbett Centre meeting was arranged.

This was attended by three students from the Corbett Centre with a member of staff and a trainee from SHIRLIE, along with the Senior Trainer. They met Catharine Niven, three assistant curators, and representatives from INTACT. Some of the issues raised were problems in getting information about what is on at the museum, the desire of the students to be able to handle museum objects, and the provision of information in alternative forms such as audio.

To address these, the museum offered to put the organisations represented at the meeting on their mailing list so that they would get copies of *What's On* and also to produce a large print version on request. Given notice, they could arrange handling sessions, and themed handling boxes are available from the outreach service for use by day centres and other community groups. They pointed out that though individual audio guides at each case might be useful, they would be very expensive. The possibility of a cassette with information about a temporary exhibition was mentioned as a cheaper alternative.

The group then took a look round some of the displays with the curators. A temporary exhibition of work by a local artist was enjoyed, as was the Natural History display where there were some specimens which could be touched, and the Railway area where a train interactive had recently been installed. Students and staff from both SHIRLIE and the Corbett Centre were keen on the idea of a Discovery Centre and felt that this would be a very useful resource which would greatly enhance their learning from museum objects.

Follow up work

A group at the SHIRLIE Project had recently carried out a survey of what their trainees thought of museums and offered to send this to us and to Inverness Museum. The points made (also referred to in *Preparing the Way*) were:

1. The writing in the museum is clear, though too small for some of our trainees.

2. Some of the writing, for instance on Geology, has words that most of us find difficult to understand.

3. There was a lot to see and learn even for those who can't read. The stuffed animals, videos and model people made it more interesting. The fact that you could touch the animals helped.

4. Staff are very helpful. They take time answering questions and never made you feel that they were eager to get rid of you. This again is helpful for those who can't read or don't understand everything but you would have to take the initiative.

5. It would be helpful if there were more activities that can be used to explain matters.

There followed a lengthy period during which progress was very slow. Contact had been made with a number of other organisations in Inverness, some of whom had responded initially, and we tried to keep them in touch with what was happening by sending reports of meetings and asking for their suggestions. However, the main contacts were with the Corbett Centre, SHIRLIE and Cantraybridge College.

One very positive development was that a trainee from the SHIRLIE Project began working at the museum transcribing reminiscence tapes. SHIRLIE has a high success rate at getting trainees into work, both paid and voluntary, and this trainee had learnt to use a word-processor while with them. She took up work at the museum as an unpaid volunteer and soon enjoyed this so much that she increased the time she spent there. By early 1998 she was doing one and a half days at the museum and another half day at a local library. Obviously this work was beneficial to the museum as they did not have the staff resources to transcribe tapes

A SHIRLIE trainee began working at the museum. This was beneficial to the museum and gave the trainee increased confidence and satisfaction.

... there was sometimes a lot of text on the screen ... it was tiring to stand while using it.

themselves, and the work gave the trainee increased confidence and satisfaction from doing a useful task as well as giving her the opportunities to meet a wider range of people.

Having seen "Talking Labels" in use at Wakefield, we contacted Horizon Marketing in Huddersfield who made these for a wide range of uses. The device was very flexible as it could be attached in several ways to a wall or showcase. It could be programmed by curators themselves with the message or information they chose, and changed as needed. INTACT obtained one which we showed to the staff at the museum.

The immediate reaction was that, for their purposes, they would prefer a version which had an individual ear-piece rather than the type which could be heard by anyone in the vicinity. INTACT obtained one of that type and sent it to the museum where it was installed in the Railway area. This already had a number of interactives, and the "Talking Label" was used to give information about the family group represented in the 19th century Waiting Room display.

Unfortunately the plans for the new discovery area had to be put on hold. Applications for outside funding were not successful, and it was a difficult time for local government services. In fact the museum suffered a cut in their budget. This was extremely depressing and frustrating at a time when the museum staff had planned a new, exciting and innovative scheme for improving their displays which would benefit everyone, and could have increased their visitor figures and educational potential.

Feedback on museum developments

As one of the original contacts at the Corbett Centre went on extended sick leave for some time, communications between her, the museum and INTACT became difficult. However, another member of staff who had continued the contact with the museum, particularly with the curator of Natural History, agreed to arrange for a group of students from the Centre to visit the Inverness Museum to give the staff feedback on some of the interactives installed since their last visit, including the "Talking Label".

On meeting the Corbett group at the museum, the first thing we looked at was an interactive computer programme on Dolphins, which was on loan from Scottish Natural Heritage. Many of the students enjoyed this, though others were less interested. Some of the comments made were that the voice was not always easy to make out, there was sometimes a lot of text on the screen which the group found rather daunting as most of them were non-readers, and that it was tiring to stand while using it. It was not easy to start the programme as the visitor had to touch a leaping dolphin twice very quickly. This programme is referred to in the section on the Computer project.

We then went to look at the Railway display where there were a number of lo-tech interactives. The train, which some of the group had not seen before, was generally liked, but some doubts were expressed about the "Indicator Panel" which was stiff to turn and some people felt that more information could have been given pictorially rather than in written form. The "Talking Label" telling about the waiting room was liked, though the message on it was quite complex. The group felt that there was scope for more use of such devices.

There had been some discussion about a possible symbol for the "Talking Label" to let people know how to use it and the Corbett

Centre students were asked for ideas. The one finally chosen shows a cartoon man smiling broadly as he uses a telephone. People have no difficulty in understanding this.

One of the Corbett Centre students wrote an account of this visit for the Centre Newsletter, saying:

We looked at the Dolphin Machine and discussed how it could be made more user-friendly. More pictures could be added to the machine's displays.

We also looked at the Railway Display and discussed with Catharine Niven about how it could be improved – we found the destination board awkward and difficult to use, and we listened to the recorded talk about the railways by means of a telephone receiver.

I personally would like more use of audio and video materials to use at home as well as in the museum. For other people with a more significant learning disability more use could be made of pictures and sound.

Afterwards there was a short meeting with the museum curator. We learnt more about the financial situation which was holding up further development of the discovery area and even delaying the final installation of a completed interactive display in the Natural History area.

How far were the aims achieved?

As far as the museum was concerned visits from groups of adults with learning disabilities are now more formalised as a result of the contacts built up between Corbett staff and museum curators. The curators had learnt more about the needs of people with learning disabilities through meeting them and talking with them. The presence of a volunteer with learning disabilities working in the museum will help this contact to continue. The Corbett staff are now more aware of the resources on offer at the museum such as handling boxes which can be borrowed. They had met some curators and feel able to approach them with requests for loans or talks to groups. When they ring to arrange a visit, they might be able to talk directly to curators they had met. Because they are known and the museum knows what to expect of the centre members, this benefits a number of the special interest groups of the members in subjects such as art and design, natural history or archaeology.

The centre staff and students appreciated being invited to take part in the consultation process for setting up the discovery area within the museum and were enthusiastic about the concept. They also gave feedback about the interactives which the museum was able to install. Many of the Corbett Centre members are now very familiar with the museum, know some of the staff by sight or even by name and feel comfortable there.

INTACT was pleased to have established some good contacts between the museum and local organisations for people with learning disabilities. While not all the organisations approached were able to reply or to offer suggestions or comments on what we were trying to do, we recognise that many of them are voluntary and so likely to be hard pressed for time and money, and would have their own priorities.

It is encouraging that the museum has been able to act on some of the suggestions made at the various meetings, such as offering a large print version of their *What's On* leaflet and including centres like Corbett on their regular mailing list. We hope that

The hope is that the people who have taken part in this project, or others similar, will be sufficiently convinced of the value of the work to want it to continue.

the links between the museum and the other organisations we worked with will continue to flourish.

On-going concerns

The most obvious of these is the problem of raising money to fund an idea like the "discovery area". This is widely recognised as a facility which schools, members of the public and many community groups would like and would make good use of. It would be a valuable educational resource for people of all ages and abilities, encouraging a multi-sensory experiential approach to learning. This is unfortunate, but is certainly not the only example of the difficulties faced by museums in trying to improve their service at a time when budgets are stretched.

Railway Interactive at Inverness Museum

The other is the difficulty of keeping contacts going. This issue arose when we lost a contact at a local special school when the person concerned took early retirement, and again when a contact at Corbett was off work for an extended period. Fortunately in the latter case, other people were able to carry on the work and the link is now probably stronger because more people are taking part.

However, particularly at a time of financial pressures on local government services, we cannot be complacent. The hope is that the people who have taken part in this project, or others similar, will be sufficiently convinced of the value of the work to want it to continue.

Finally, a piece of good news – another interactive display is being installed in the Railway area. It consists of a model of a set of shelves in a left luggage area, with assorted luggage on them. Visitors will be able to lift a flap forming a fishing bag or a carpet bag, for example, and find the sort of things that might have been carried inside it on the Highland Railway.

Note

The "Talking Label" tried out at Inverness Museum and Art Gallery was supplied by Horizon Marketing of Huddersfield.

Stop Press

As this report goes to press, INTACT has been told that there is a possibility that funding will now be found and Inverness Museum and Art Gallery will be able to go ahead with their plans for the discovery area. If so, this is indeed good news.

People with sensory and intellectual impairments face barriers which prevent them from participating in the life of museums and galleries. These barriers for the most part concern accessing and engaging with the works displayed and are therefore directly linked to interpretation.
Rebecca McGinnis[1]

Although some of the other pilot projects were at museums which included art works in their collections, namely at Inverness, Dundee and Kelvingrove in Glasgow, INTACT wanted to work specifically in the visual arts. One reason for this is that many people with learning disabilities enjoy looking at works of art and also taking part in creative art workshops of various kinds in day centres, colleges and through organisations like the Project Ability Centre for Developmental Arts in Glasgow.

The project looked at a number of ways of making different kinds of art more accessible to people with learning difficulties. INTACT worked with staff from the National Galleries of Scotland (NGS) and with the Fruitmarket Gallery who show temporary exhibitions of contemporary art, including photography.

INTACT's partners:

Michael Cassin, Head of Education
National Galleries of Scotland

Siobhan Dougherty, Education Officer
National Galleries of Scotland

Marc Lambert, Interpretation Officer
Fruitmarket Gallery, Edinburgh

Staff, students and centre members from a number of day centres, colleges and special schools in Edinburgh

Kenny Bean, Photographer

Aims of Visual Arts Project

National Galleries of Scotland:

1. to make day centre and FE college special needs department staff aware of the services and facilities offered by NGS, and the strategies employed in the different Galleries to make best use of their educational resources

2. to make clear the distinction between using a National Gallery with a permanent collection of historical works of art and visiting galleries with no permanent collections but which mount temporary exhibitions

3. to make contact with day centre and college staff in person and to build up their confidence in leading small groups of their students round the Galleries themselves

INTACT:

1. to encourage contacts between galleries' staff and organisations for people with learning disabilities

2. to make people with learning disabilities and staff who work with them more aware of the resources available in galleries, such as the National Galleries of Scotland and others showing contemporary art such as the Fruitmarket Gallery

3. to explore some of the alternative means of access to gallery interpretation

There were really three aspects to this pilot project. While these did not precisely conform to the aims, they were covered by them:

1. working with Michael Cassin and Siobhan Dougherty at the National Galleries of Scotland (NGS), that is the National

Centres were trying to get away from their clients' being seen in the community in large 'institutionalised' groups.

Gallery of Scotland, the Scottish National Portrait Gallery and the Scottish National Gallery of Modern Art

2. a photography workshop with the Fruitmarket Gallery during the Thomas Joshua Cooper Exhibition

3. inviting groups to try the audio guides available at the National Gallery of Scotland and the Fruitmarket Gallery (during the Mag Collection exhibition) and give feedback on their use

These three aspects will be considered in turn.

1. National Galleries of Scotland

An initial approach was made to Michael Cassin to discuss what could be done. Having read his paper, *Are you having a nice time?*[2] it was fascinating to see him in action with a group of school pupils and the response he elicited from them. It seemed likely that a similar approach of helping visitors to relate to the pictures, to interact with them and to look closely for clues about what the artist is communicating would work with people with learning disabilities.

However, there was a concern about creating a demand which the Galleries Education Staff would be unable to meet because of other demands for their services in covering three collections at three sites. This means that different strategies need to be employed in particular contexts. It has been one of the aims of this project to develop these strategies and make them more generally known and available to college and day centre staff working with people with learning disabilities.

A meeting was arranged with a group of interested staff from day centres and college special needs departments, to discuss possible ways to make gallery visits more interesting and rewarding for centre members and students with learning disabilities. Eleven people attended and there were apologies from people who would have liked to come but were unable to do so at the last minute.

The group were able to see Michael Cassin's approach of drawing out ideas of what the picture was about and what the artist was trying to do. He suggested that staff in the group could use these techniques with their own students when visiting the galleries. He also spoke about what the gallery staff were able to offer to students from day centres and college special needs departments. If they knew in advance about the requirements of a visiting group of people with learning disabilities, they could be flexible in responding to their needs.

Subsequently two or three of the group were able to arrange visits and talks by gallery staff for their students. Where this had happened, everyone had enjoyed the experience. In many cases these visits inspired the students to produce their own art work. One enthusiast arranged talks for his students at all three of the National Galleries.

However, others in the group said that they would feel uncomfortable and quite intimidated at the idea of talking with their students about a work of art in a public space like a gallery. They felt too that the size of group the Galleries were prepared to give talks to (normally 10 – 12) was too many. Their students would get more from smaller groups, such as 3 or 4, as they would be less inhibited about asking questions and there would be fewer distractions.

Additionally, centres were trying to get away from their clients' being seen in the community in large 'institutionalised' groups. Issues of fitting visits to Galleries into an already full timetable and availability of sufficient staff and transport to take groups out, were mentioned as possible problems.

There had been a few suggestions that themed talks might be a good idea, and this resulted in a visit by the staff group to the National Gallery of Modern Art for a talk by Siobhan Dougherty, another member of the Education staff. This time the group looked at a number of portraits. They discussed what kind of people the subjects were, what some sculptures represented and what they were made of, and why the artist presented himself the way he did in a self portrait.

The feedback from this was that the group found the visit very useful. Though they had all enjoyed Michael Cassin's session with some of the pictures at the National Gallery and had found his approach very helpful, many of them identified the works in the Gallery of Modern Art as more immediately approachable for their clients. The Scottish Gallery of Modern Art building and collection are perhaps less intimidating and this could have been a factor in their feeling that their students would feel more comfortable there. We therefore arranged another meeting with Siobhan for a time when *Surrealism and After*, the Gabrielle Keiller Collection was on display.

Meantime, a group from a day centre in Dunfermline came to see the Keiller Collection and another exhibition which featured two video presentations. Although this group had not been able to do any preparatory work, the staff who came were prepared to talk about the works with the students and encourage them to react and express opinions. There was a good staff/student ratio so people were able to go round in small groups.

As the exhibition was so diverse, most of the group found something that they could relate to. It was interesting to see how their lack of preconceptions about "what is art?" enabled them to respond. It was a good exercise in careful looking to work out what the very varied paintings and sculptures represented and why they were presented in that way. The students were almost all fascinated by *Endlessly*, a video installation by young Scottish artists Dalziel and Scullion.

Unfortunately, only a handful of people were able to come to a second talk by Siobhan Dougherty. However, those who did were given the chance to ask questions and express concerns, such as feeling uncomfortable speaking with a group of students in a public place. Siobhan was very reassuring about this as she does it regularly. She also gave some advice about trying to use the larger rooms rather than corridor areas where a group could inconvenience other visitors, and borrowing folding stools to help keep the group together and focused on the work being discussed.

This time she suggested looking at things like surfaces and textures, the atmosphere evoked by a work and how to look at something three dimensional. She also mentioned that the galleries had postcard-sized reproductions of some of the works of art on display and that the Central Fine Art Library had a collection of slides which library members could borrow. These could be used for pre- or post-visit work.

As so many of the original group were not present, we agreed that it would be useful to put together some guidelines for staff bringing students to the galleries and send this out to them. After Siobhan had checked

It was interesting to see how their lack of preconceptions about "what is art?" enabled them to respond.

"I wish it was morning again so that I could do it all over again".

the draft, this was duly issued (see page 105).

2. The Fruitmarket Gallery

This Gallery already had a reputation for working with community groups and people with disabilities, arranging workshops in connection with exhibitions and for having a very flexible attitude to interpretation. It had hosted an Interpretation seminar in November 1996.

Photography Workshop

The original idea for working with the Fruitmarket came from contact with Amanda Hogg, the Interpretation Officer at that time, who had come to the first talk by Michael Cassin. However, because she left in the summer of 1997, this was put on hold until Marc Lambert started in post.

After discussion, the idea for photographic workshops emerged. A week of these had already been arranged; ten sessions for school pupils in conjunction with the Thomas Joshua Cooper Exhibition *Where the Rivers Flow*. INTACT was able to negotiate for two of these sessions to be for pupils at special schools, and for them to have the first choice of times. A number of special schools in and around Edinburgh were offered these sessions on a 'first come, first served' basis. The first two to reply were duly offered places. INTACT met Marc Lambert and Kenny Bean, the photographer who was doing the sessions, to discuss the format.

As we were not sure about the capabilities of the pupils, we decided to go for making negative prints directly from slides of natural objects. We were concerned that if they tried to expose film to make negatives and then print from them (as was arranged for the mainstream pupils), there might not be time to complete the process. As well as making their own photographs, we wanted them to see the work in the exhibition.

The two schools concerned were visited so that we could meet some of the pupils who might come and the staff who would accompany them. Everyone was very enthusiastic at the prospect of developing and printing their own pictures. One of the schools, which was in the process of installing a dark room but had not yet got it up and running, was looking forward to picking up ideas.

Each session started with the pupils looking at a selection of natural objects which included leaf skeletons, feathers, cast snakeskins and seaweed. They were encouraged to choose small pieces and make these up into slides which were then projected onto the wall so that they could see the details and structures enlarged. Kenny then pointed out that, while fascinating to look at, these images disappeared as soon as the light was turned off, and so introduced the idea of capturing an image. This was done by producing a sheet of light sensitive paper which he had exposed at a window with some items on top of it.

The pupils were then introduced to the dark room where enlargers had been set up with prepared slides of similar natural objects. The process of exposing and developing was explained and they started off by making test exposures. Each pupil chose the appropriate exposure for his or her slide before developing, fixing, washing and drying the result. They were all intrigued by the idea of counting in 'elephants' to time the exposures and fascinated to see the images appear in the developing solution. Everyone managed at least two prints to take home and a few did more.

All of them very obviously enjoyed the experience, one girl said:

I wish it was morning again so that I could do it all over again.

and many commented on how quickly the time had passed.

The teachers who came along said they had picked up a number of ideas for activities with their pupils from the exercise and both schools hope to enter work for a local photographic competition. Teachers commented on the degree of concentration displayed by pupils who normally had a very short attention span, and on the amount of conversation and discussion the sessions generated. This is an important benefit for pupils who may have problems expressing themselves.

Teachers commented on the degree of concentration displayed by pupils who normally had a very short attention span ...

3. Audio guides

National Gallery of Scotland

In the summer of 1997, the National Gallery of Scotland at the Mound, Edinburgh, introduced Acoustiguides to provide "informed, detailed and anecdotal" information about the Gallery's greatest works in the permanent collection. Some of the commentaries, written by the Keeper and Head of Education, were narrated by gallery staff and others by well known Scottish actors. The system consists of a lightweight hand-held unit with a keypad which gives visitors access to up to two hours of information in English, French or Italian.

For the ordinary visitor, the system is very flexible and easy to use. There is no set route so that people can wander round at their own speed and get recorded information on any work with the numbered symbol, simply by keying in that number. When they have heard as much as they want about one work, they can stop the guide and move on to another work. It is a great advantage to be able to stand back from a picture (or even to sit!) and listen to information about it, rather than trying to read a label or a guidebook while looking at the picture.

INTACT was able to arrange for a group of students with cerebral palsy from a Capability Scotland day centre to visit the Gallery and use the Acoustiguides. Three of the students were wheelchair users, and some had limited grip which made it awkward to key in numbers or keep the hand-held unit close enough to the ear. But they were all keen to do as much as possible for themselves and had strong ideas about the works they wanted information about. As a member of staff wrote after the visit

All in all the students enjoyed the experience and appreciated learning more about the works of art that they were looking at. Even with the assistance of the staff present this still gave our students more choice and independence in this outing.

"It is nice to be able to hear the information when you can't read".

"I liked to know what the person was thinking".

As all the students were interested in art, though unable to read, this opened up a whole new experience other than just looking at the pictures. The benefits of increased choice and independence for people with this kind of communication disability cannot be quantified but are clearly valuable.

Fruitmarket Gallery

The Mag Collection of image based British art from the last two decades of the 20th century was exhibited at the Fruitmarket Gallery in early 1998. Hand held audio guides containing recordings of artists talking about some of the works were available during the exhibition.

The information provided on these audio guides was often quite personal to the artist and in no way was telling visitors "about" the works on display. The information was intriguing but very variable; it was especially interesting when the artist was talking. Sometimes this information repeated what was on the label and this would be helpful for those who find it difficult to read.

Two groups were invited from different day centres to look at the exhibition and try the audio guides. One was a small group of two students and a member of staff. The other was a member of staff and six students and we were joined by a lecturer from the FE college that the students would have attended for an Art class if they had not come to the gallery.

The reactions from both groups were similar, though it was easier to keep track of the smaller group and get opinions from those students. All felt that the guides added something to the experience of looking at the works in the collection. They found some of the language was quite difficult, using abstract words like 'concept'. Some students found it difficult to key in the numbers and needed help, and some had to be encouraged to look at the pictures while listening to the information.

Some comments from students were:

It is nice to be able to hear the information when you can't read.

and:

I liked to know what the person was thinking.

The staff present felt that everyone gained something from seeing the exhibition and using the guides, and agreed that audio was a useful way for their clients to get information. However, they made a number of suggestions about the language level. They were not sure quite what audience the commentaries were aimed at and felt that it was often too abstract for non art-specialists.

They suggested that such guides might be more use to their students, and possibly to non art-specialist members of the public, if they referred more directly to things that people could see, such as the colours or shapes. Or they could pose questions as to why an artist had put certain images together or what s/he wanted the viewer to feel.

How far have the aims of the Visual Arts Project been met?

INTACT is very grateful to Siobhan Dougherty and Marc Lambert who sent us detailed comments on the project, to the staff from the day centres and colleges who attended talks and brought groups, and for the direct response from the centre members, students and pupils who took part in visits and workshops.

National Galleries of Scotland

Through this series of talks and visits, and the exchange of information between the Galleries staff and centre/college staff, we felt that the aims of NGS had largely been met.

Siobhan Dougherty said that she had learnt something of the problems faced by people with learning and communication disabilities through talking to the staff who worked with them and by visiting a day centre following the invitation of a member of the staff group.

She found it useful to have the names of the group members as contacts whom she knew were interested in helping their students to have access to works of art, and as a possible group to consult about access for people with learning disabilities in the future. As a result she hoped that they would be more aware of the facilities which NGS could offer, but also to understand the distinction between the National Galleries with their permanent collections and other galleries which mount temporary exhibitions.

Her recommendations to staff bringing groups to the galleries include:

- staff bringing a group should be familiar with the layout of the building and know where to find the works that their students wish to look at

- as rooms can be temporarily closed or works may be on loan, it is advisable to check whether specific works are available, or to have alternatives planned

- it is important that all students and accompanying staff understand that none of the works of art on display may be touched as many of them are fragile, or the surface may be damaged by contact.

She also mentioned that special arrangements could be made through the Education Department for groups visiting special exhibitions which have an admission charge, provided two weeks notice is given. In any case it is advisable for staff bringing a group to give at least a week's notice with details of the size of the group, the time and length of visit and the gallery to be visited.

Although it seemed that, on the whole, both staff and students from the day centres and colleges found the works in the Scottish National Gallery of Modern Art more immediately enjoyable, we hope that they will continue to persevere with both the National Gallery of Scotland and the Scottish National Portrait Gallery. If people with learning disabilities are not able to see various styles from different periods, they will be less able to judge what they like.

There are frequent temporary exhibitions in both galleries, such as *Stars of Stage and Screen* which was at the Scottish National Portrait Gallery in early 1998, which offer the chance to visit and look at a very specific topic. Alternatively, the idea of themed visits, mentioned by one of the centre/college staff group, might be a possibility though these would involve some staff preparation.

Day Centres and Colleges

The group of day centre and college staff also supplied feedback both as the project progressed and at the end. Some of the reservations many of the group had about talking about works of art in public have already been mentioned, but the main concerns for many were the timetabling, transport and staff problems presented by bringing a group to one of the Galleries. At least one of the centres and one college group are trying to build some time into the programme for such visits. Often the summer is a better time for visits as the timetable is more flexible then.

Centre users are now given more choice about their activities. One person's programme for the week can include sessions at the day centre, courses at college and time spent on other activities. Obviously more choice means that centre users have to make a positive decision to visit a gallery rather than just tagging along with a group. This in turn means that the gallery must try to make visits enjoyable and satisfying so that people want to go again, and even tell others about it so that they opt to go next time.

Shortage of staff, perhaps because of illness, sometimes resulted in the last minute cancellation of an arranged visit. This could also happen because of problems with transport.

Some staff felt that the Galleries' guidelines about the size of groups to whom they would offer talks by education staff were inappropriately large. This gave rise to a conflict of interest, given the pressures on gallery education staff time. We hope that this may be solved in part by centre and college staff gaining the confidence to discuss pictures with their students in public, and possibly by more flexibility by the gallery staff regarding the size of groups.

Some day centre staff enquired about work sheets, but the general feeling was that these were not appropriate for adults. Though not possible for everyone, it was felt that more time given to preparation, such as a preliminary visit by staff themselves, perhaps picking up some postcard reproductions or identifying certain works for students to concentrate on, would be a more useful approach.

INTACT

Looking again at the fairly modest aims stated earlier, these were effectively achieved.

Contacts

While there were contacts previously in that day centre staff were already bringing small groups to art galleries, we have tried to formalise this contact. We did this by arranging talks by NGS staff to day centre and college special needs department staff and by arranging a number of visits by students and centre members to look at particular exhibitions or try audio guides. Even on the most informal level, this has helped to break down some of the barriers faced by people with learning disabilities.

Both sides felt that they gained from these meetings:

- gallery staff gained more insight into the problems people with learning disabilities have in learning about the works on display and getting more stimulation when visiting

- the centre/college staff gained confidence in talking to their groups about the displays

As Marc Lambert wrote:

Through working with INTACT, the Fruitmarket Gallery has been able to make contact with new groups and broaden the scope of the outreach and education programme.

He noted the comments made by the groups who tried the audio guides and agreed with them, but pointed out that the Gallery also offers 'Live Guides' who are available either by booking or on demand, and that the Gallery staff are sensitive to the differing needs of the various groups that make use of this facility.

We now have a core list of day centre and college staff who are interested in arranging gallery visits for their students and this has been passed on to the galleries (National and Fruitmarket) and added to their regular mailing lists.

Raising awareness of gallery resources

Through the meetings mentioned above, staff from centres and colleges are now more aware of the resources offered by the galleries, such as what is on display, what is available in terms of visits and talks and the procedure for booking. They are now sent regular mailing about what's on and this can be displayed in centres and colleges to help students make informed choices about what to visit.

Alternative means of gallery interpretation

Again following the meetings mentioned above, a number of day centre staff have felt more confident about bringing groups to visit galleries and more able to help their students understand something of the works of art on display. Those who have had the confidence to talk about the works to small groups of their students have found that this was not as daunting as they had feared, though keeping the attention of a group can be a problem.

Invited groups have tried out audio guides and the general feeling is that these are a useful additional means of getting information across to people with learning disabilities. The level of language is still an issue as most of the existing audio guides in use in galleries are designed for people who are interested in art and know something about it already. While there are unlikely to be commercial guides designed for people with learning disabilities, there might be scope for interested staff (from day centres or from a gallery) to record ideas on normal cassette tape about exhibitions and perhaps make this available to visiting groups.

The groups of special school pupils, who attended the photographic workshops in connection with an exhibition, acquired some understanding of the process of developing and printing photographs. They also gained considerable enjoyment and sense of participation from the experience.

Conclusion

While everyone concerned learnt a great deal from the different aspects of this project, there are some anxieties about the continuation of the contacts made during it. There are considerable pressures on staff time in centres and colleges and in gallery education or interpretation departments so that it may be difficult to maintain these links.

Given the positive response of those involved in the work, we remain optimistic. But much will depend on the galleries continuing to send out their *What's On* information, and day centre/college staff being prepared to give them regular feedback on visits to exhibitions.

References

1. *Making sense of Art* R McGinnis paper presented at the *Interpretation Seminar* Fruitmarket Gallery, Edinburgh (20/11/96)

2. *Are you having a nice time?* M Cassin in *Object Lessons* edit S Mitchell **HMSO** (1996)

As more people with learning disabilities now live in the community they have a greater need for accessible information about all aspects of life, including ideas about leisure activities.

There is little point in increasing the range of what is available for people with learning disabilities if they do not know about such services, cannot get to them or do not feel comfortable when they get there.
Building Expectations – Opportunities and Services for People with a Learning Disability (1996)[1]

The idea behind this exercise came originally from two sources. One was the North East Museums Service/Museums and Galleries Disability Association Conference in Newcastle which included input from people with learning disabilities who had been consulted about improving access to the Hancock Museum. They had suggested that there was need for improvement both in the design of leaflets and posters and other publicity material, and in their distribution.

The other was increasing awareness of the problems of print size, style, colour and the background design in museum text and labels. The same problems were also shown in the design of publicity materials such as leaflets and posters.

William Kirby, chair of MAGDA, in *Access to Museums by Adult Learners with Disabilities* mentions finding out about

extensive facilities for print-handicapped visitors which were seriously under-used because people with disabilities were not aware of their existence[2]

This is a fundamental problem.

As more people with learning disabilities now live in the community they have a greater need for accessible information about all aspects of life, including ideas about leisure activities.

INTACT was advised by:

Disability Scotland

Enable

Scottish Working Group on Information Services for People with Disabilities

Dr Helen Sinclair, Principal Education Officer, Tyne and Wear Museums

Isabel Churcher, Head of Museum Service, Hereford City Museums

Elaine Greig
City of Edinburgh Museums and Galleries

Christine Thompson, Disability Liaison Officer, National Museums of Scotland

Aims

- to look at ways of improving the information supplied by museums to people with learning (and other) disabilities to let them know:

a) what is on and ...

b) ... what facilities are available both in general and specifically to help those with disabilities

- to look at how this information is distributed and whether this could be improved.

The Process

Publicity leaflets for museums, galleries and historic sites are easily obtained at other such places along with libraries and theatres where there are often racks of them. They can also be found regularly in places like cafés, restaurants and guest houses, as well as tourist information centres. Thus it was not hard to accumulate a fair collection and to look at them critically to judge their usefulness for people with disabilities.

If museums provide leaflets which, at least in the first place, have information about their collection and the facilities available in a format accessible to all, this is preferable. However, it is sometimes helpful for an organisation to provide additional information for people with disabilities, such as facts about physical access (if this is very different from access for the non-disabled) and to offer alternative formats like large print or an audio version for people with a visual impairment.

Examples of material produced by various museums around the country were found to have considerable shortcomings even for the ordinary visitor.

Readers who wish to follow up this topic are advised to consult the publications listed at the end of this section which is simply a summary of other people's findings but with an emphasis on the particular needs of people with learning disabilities.

Formats

As publicity material comes in different formats, often each with a different purpose, it might be as well to mention some of the most common.

1. Simple leaflets to state that an attraction is there. These are often flat, unfolded and can come in various sizes (for example A5, or A4 folded x 2 or x 3) and may be printed on one or both sides. These tend to give the most basic information only and may be used to publicise a special exhibition or an event.

2. Leaflets giving more information about the collection and facilities. These will often be a size like A4 folded x 3, even A3 folded x 6 (both resulting in 21 x 10 cm, which fits easily into a common size of rack), or A4 folded x 2. These are sometimes used as a regularly up-dated *What's On* and may appear at intervals from every month to every quarter. In this case they will give priority to new and forthcoming displays, but will usually have some information about a permanent collection as well.

3. Posters. These can vary in size, but usually will have the same level of information as the simple leaflets in 1 above. In fact, the same design is sometimes used for both, with the smaller version being used as a 'flyer'.

4. Orientation leaflets or plans which are supplied inside a museum. These come in a variety of formats, but usually include a map or plan to show the location of different displays and the facilities offered. They may include suggested 'Highlights' tours for visitors with limited time.

Obviously other formats are appropriate in different contexts.

The main problems that were identified

The following criticisms were made by a number of groups of people with learning disabilities and by people who work with them:

1. very small print, often over a drawing or picture which added to the problems in reading

2. general lack of clarity, which could be overcome by using simpler type faces and language

3. lack of clear information about how to find the museum/gallery, for example by providing a map or giving information about buses or where to park

4. not enough clear information about facilities in general such as toilets, café, or about wheelchair access, lifts or induction loops for those with disabilities. There were some examples of the use of symbols, but these were not consistent and sometimes the logos were very small

5. poor distribution of information to people with disabilities. Often leaflets are in places like other museums or galleries, libraries and theatres which appeal mainly to those who already go to museums. They should also be available in community centres, day centres, doctors' surgeries and other such places

6. variable quality of information about the collections and displays or the availability of guided tours or talks.

The Informability Manual makes similar points:

Design features such as printing text on top of images, or positioning columns or lines of text too close together, can create barriers to comprehension.[3]

Easily recognisable symbols as used by Tyne and Wear Museums

It also recommends short line lengths; short, clearly separated chunks of text; simple words and short sentences without being patronising; and the use of symbols, illustrations, diagrams and photographs to supplement text.

It must be emphasised that, though many people with learning disabilities cannot read, they like to be able to understand enough independently from a leaflet or poster to know if they are interested in a particular attraction and might want to pay a visit.

They should be able, perhaps through the use of graphics and symbols, to find out what they will be able to see and do, and if there are facilities such as a café, a shop, accessible toilets, audio guides etc. Help might be required to find out about opening times, charges (if any) or public transport, but it is important that they themselves can get the information needed to make the initial choice whether they think there is something of interest to them or not.

However, as it is unrealistic to expect many museums to provide information specifically for people with learning disabilities (see below for one example), we have made suggestions which we hope will improve leaflets and publicity materials for everyone, including those with physical or sensory disabilities.

INTACT, along with those we consulted, feel that inclusive leaflets, suitable for all visitors, are the best solution. Many people who may not consider themselves to be disabled would welcome information about parking or lifts. Everyone benefits from clear print in a reasonable size of type, and designers should be aware of the problems faced by those who might be colour-blind (about 1 in 12 of the male population have some degree of colour abnormality).

However in some cases, for example a large institution with a complex site or a group of linked museums and galleries, it might be more appropriate to produce a guide for visitors with disabilities which would cover all aspects and could be made available in alternative formats such as Braille, large print or in an audio version. Where this is planned, it is essential to consult people with disabilities to make sure that all the information required is included and that it is accurate. For example, Gateshead Access Panel recommend trying out a design on the intended audience before publishing tens of thousands of copies.

Museum Information which would help people with disabilities

Ideally, this should include:

1. how to reach the building, with a plan as well as public transport and parking information

2. days and times of opening, including the last admission time if appropriate, as well as charges if any, and concession rates

3. a brief description of the type of displays the museum offers in everyday language including what temporary exhibitions will be on. This means it will have to be updated regularly

4. what facilities are available; this means information about access for wheelchair users (if available, otherwise a statement that this is not possible), whether there are lifts, toilets (including accessible ones), induction loops, information in Braille, audio or large print, café/restaurant, shop and if there are guided tours, tactile tours or tours in sign language, or audio guides, and if guide dogs admitted

5. access logos, if used, should be large enough to be easily recognised, used consistently and preferably in a logical order from the entrance, indicating flat access, a ramp or platform lift, then moving on to facilities such as induction loops and accessible toilets and ending with general facilities like a shop or café

6. a telephone number to ask for further information, including minicom if available, and a statement that information is available in alternative formats such as audio, Braille or large print

7. a statement that people with disabilities are welcome and staff will do their best to help

8. an indication of any outreach work, lectures or workshops if these are offered and a number to ring for more information

9. orientation leaflets or plans available inside the museum should include a plan of the interior with facilities clearly marked and more detailed information on the various areas and displays. For people with learning disabilities, the use of colour coding and/or symbols would be useful.

Posters, which may be advertising special events or exhibitions, need basic readability plus the information in 1, 2 and 5 above and the information in 4 and 5 relevant to the exhibition in clear symbol form.

Anyone wanting specific guidelines for providing written information for people with learning disabilities should consult *The Informability Manual* pages 39 and 40. However, for most purposes, the suggestions on page 12, to help people with poor literacy, will be enough. These are that printed material should be:

- in plain language
- as concise as possible
- in clear type (but not too large)

On the same page, under *Design and Layout*, the Manual states:

Illustrations, photographs, cartoons and diagrams can help keep text to a minimum, make the message clearer, and the

Printed material should be:

- **in plain language**
- **as concise as possible**
- **in clear type**

When lettering is orientated differently from the reading direction it magnifies any reading difficulty as each letter must be processed separately. Unfortunately …

v e r t i c a l t e x t i s n o t u n c o m m o n

material more attractive and user-friendly. This is true for most audiences, not just for those with literacy problems.[4]

Isabel Churcher, in her very comprehensive *Guidelines for Effective Museum Leaflets*[5] lists ten key design variables and gives "do"s and "don't"s for each of them.

These variables are:

1. title
2. logo
3. style/image of museum
4. typeface and size
5. format of information
6. number and use of colours
7. use of illustrations
8. size and shape of leaflet
9. paper type and weight
10. the front cover

She also gives recommendations for the contents. These cover aspects like 'politically correct' language, legible type faces and sizes, and promoting specific features such as the educational service or showing pictures of children and mixed generation families enjoying themselves. Examples are given of both good and bad features from actual museum leaflets.

James Holmes-Siedle in Chapter 6 of *Barrier-free Design*[6] gives clear recommendations about font style and size as well as explaining the importance of contrast (text/background) and orientation. The latter, referring to when lettering is orientated differently from the reading direction, magnifies any reading difficulty as each letter must be processed separately. Unfortunately, vertical text is not uncommon as a feature of leaflet design.

How to improve the situation

Museum staff could be more aware of the needs of people with disabilities as a target audience. However this is not easy as there are often seen to be greater priorities. When an Access Audit is carried out, this could well be one of the issues identified.

Communication links between different members of staff within an institution could be strengthened. A leaflet or poster produced for a particular exhibition should be checked by someone with a knowledge of access to ensure that it meets the required guidelines. This can be hard enough within one museum or gallery, never mind between all those in the same local group, or even between the different departments of a local authority, but the long-term benefits of a combined strategy are considerable.

Staff within a museum (or better still within a group of museums, or a local authority) could co-operate in producing a design brief for accessible publicity leaflets and posters. Then, as these are updated or replaced, they will fulfil the necessary requirements. In the case of a group of museums, they could create a group image, for example as is done in Tyne and Wear, and probably save on costs.

Isabel Churcher mentions the advantages of developing a strong logo or style in creating a positive image which people will recognise. This is particularly useful where a number of museums in a locality are associated and creates a 'brand image' which emphasises the unity of the service as a whole.

The purpose of any publicity leaflet must be clear as there is a limit to the amount of information which can be included. However some information, possibly in the form of approved symbols, should always be provided for people with disabilities as well as a contact number to find out more.

The Arts Council of England's *Guidelines for Marketing to Disabled People* (1993)[7] stresses the need for consultation, avoiding negative messages, targeting advertising and looking at pricing policy. It suggests that access leaflets should be upbeat and welcoming but also realistic. It is important to use appropriate language and to use access symbols correctly.

It emphasises the need to be honest; wrong or incomplete information is of no use. Rather than using a vague message like "partial disabled access", spell out any potential problems, such as a ramp which is steeper than recommended or the existence of unavoidable steps. If people are aware of specific problems in advance, they can take the decision as to whether they will be able to manage, with or without assistance.

MAGDA, in its publication *Sharing the Wisdom of Age*[8] recommends that the services on offer should be described as fully as possible and advises:

do not be afraid of saying what a museum lacks because this can be as important as knowing what is available when planning a visit.

It is essential that, no matter how good the publicity leaflets are, staff answering questions about access have full and accurate information to give out. If a telephone, fax or minicom number is given on a leaflet for visitors to ring for more information on access, it is vital that any potential questions can be answered quickly and accurately. *Guidelines for Marketing to Disabled People* suggests that:

a full, fair and frank access leaflet is a vital marketing tool[9]

and that it should be used as a reference by staff answering queries as well as being made available with other literature or mailed to appropriate organisations. Such staff must be fully trained and aware of all potential user needs.

Publicity Outlets

Many people with learning and other disabilities do not see publicity leaflets or posters giving information about museums and galleries because they do not go to places where these are distributed at present.

If museums want to widen their visitor profile, they will have to put information in places visited by those who are not already museum goers. Some ideas from people with disabilities, and organisations working with them, include:

- sending leaflets to day centres for people with physical or learning disabilities, and also to residential accommodation
- contacting relevant organisations and arranging for space in their newsletters
- using existing facilities such as talking newspapers
- targeting particular groups for special interest exhibitions, such as organisations for people with visual impairment if touch tours are on offer
- putting up posters or sending leaflets to community centres, sports centres and places where people go for adult basic education. Other possibilities are shopping centres and launderettes

It is essential that, no matter how good the publicity leaflets are, staff answering questions about access have full and accurate information to give out.

In addition to these ideas, the National Information Forum in *How to Provide Information Well* (1996)[10] suggests Health Centres, Citizens' Advice Bureaux and Social Services and Benefits Agency's Offices.

Obviously, sending out more leaflets and posters has a cost, so careful evaluation of distribution to non-traditional places would be needed to establish its effectiveness. Some suggested monitoring and evaluation strategies are given in Isabel Churcher's paper.

Potential Difficulties

- lack of money to update leaflets or to send them out where there is no guarantee of response

- problems of co-ordinating different departments in order to redesign leaflets

- different agendas of people taking part in the process, such as designers, curators, publicity staff and those concerned with disability issues

Alternative media

Some museums and galleries produce information in audio form , usually in conjunction with a local 'Talking Newspaper' service. Edinburgh City Museums & Galleries are on the computer Cap-Info system, which is available free in most of the City's libraries.

Disability Scotland is setting up a data base, DS-DATA, of the information formerly in directories which includes a section on Arts, Sport & Leisure.

A number of organisations for people with disabilities, such as Family Advice and Information Resource (FAIR), Scottish Down's Syndrome Association (SDSA) and Capability Scotland have newsletters and are very willing to carry information about displays particularly relevant to their members.

The Royal Museum in Edinburgh had a computer visitor information system on trial in April 1997. This included information about facilities for people with disabilities. Feedback was very positive, with many visitors saying it should be a permanent feature.

Other suggestions for publicising special exhibitions are local radio and local free newspapers. Advertisements on local buses have been used, but they lose credibility if they continue after an exhibition has closed.

Ways Forward

Enabling Information[11] which looked at the broad picture of providing all kinds of information for people with disabilities, recommends:

- raising the awareness of disability among service providers of all types

- collaboration, multi-agency working and networking at a local level

- the development of standards, which should be the responsibility of an advisory body composed of disabled people, carers, and their representatives, together with others of appropriate experience

INTACT fully agrees with these recommendations; raising awareness of the needs of people with learning disabilities is one of our principal objects. We support, and have suggested earlier in this report, the advantages of agencies and departments working together, and we would welcome the setting of standards and guidelines for the provision of information for people with disabilities.

However, we would strongly recommend that people with learning disabilities would be represented on the advisory panel to make sure that their specific needs were recognised.

References

1. *Building Expectations – Opportunities and Services for People with a Learning Disability* **Mental Health Foundation** (1996)

2. *Access to Museums by Adult Learners with Disabilities* W Kirby in *Museums and the Education of Adults* edit Chadwick and Stannett **NIACE** (1995)

3. *The Informability Manual* W Gregory **HMSO** (1996)

4. Gregory (1996) op cit

5. *Guidelines for Effective Museum Leaflets* I Churcher MA Thesis **University of Leicester** (1995) unpublished

6. *Barrier-free design* James Holmes-Siedle, **Butterworth Architecture** (1996) Chapter 6 on *Access to advertising and publicity material*

7. *Guidelines for Marketing to Disabled People* **Arts Council of England** (1993)

8. *Sharing the Wisdom of Age* **MAGDA** (1995)

9. **Arts Council of England** op cit

10. *How to Provide Information Well* **The National Information Forum** (1996)

11. *Enabling Information* **Scottish Working Group on Information Services for People with Disabilities** (1995)

Also consulted:

Making it easy first **People First**

Making Reading Easier **Basic Skills Agency** (1992)

Guidelines for Printed Information **Tyne & Wear Museums**

Guidelines for Producing Information in Large Print **Lothian Coalition of Disabled People** (1995)

Designing to Enable **Gateshead Access Panel** (1997)

Access to Information Minutes of the **MAGDA** Meeting at the British Museum (June 1997)

We must avoid creating a world designed only for those with mild or moderate disabilities, instead of one designed for those with no learning disabilities at all. Our conviction is – and evidence shows – that people with the most severe disabilities also seek friends, choice, education, homes of their own and activities suitable to their age, interests and talents ... There is a real concern that their needs will be marginalised in the general thrust of services towards greater integration and normalisation.
Mental Health Foundation Inquiry Report *Building Expectations: Opportunities and Services for People with a Learning Disability* 1996.

INTACT felt that the idea of improving access for people with such severe impairments would be very worthwhile, as well as a major challenge.

This project began through a contact with Loretto Lambe, PAMIS Project Director based at the White Top Research Unit at Dundee University. PAMIS (Profound and Multiple Impairment Service) is concerned with the needs of people with a profound learning disability who also have physical disabilities and/or severe visual or hearing impairments, and offers support to parents and carers by providing information and practical help.

However, as the pilot project evolved, other organisations took part and there were a number of strands to the work.

INTACT's partners:

Project Director and staff at PAMIS and the Parents' and Supporters' Group

Professor James Hogg of The White Top Research Unit, Department of Social Work, Dundee University

Staff at City of Dundee Arts and Heritage

Staff and centre users at the White Top Centre

Staff and centre users at Dudhope Centre

Staff at Verdant Works, Dundee Heritage Trust

Aims

- to try to improve access for people with profound and multiple learning difficulties (PMLD) to museums, galleries and historic sites, by providing activities based on the objects, art works or site which would be meaningful, would enable them to participate in the experience and would add to their enjoyment

- to encourage contacts between staff from local museums and galleries with PAMIS (including parents and supporters), the White Top Research Unit at Dundee University and White Top Centre staff and users, particularly in the development of multi-sensory displays

- to raise awareness among parents and carers of those with PMLD to the possibilities of visiting museums, galleries or historic buildings as a rewarding leisure activity for their sons and daughters

The Process

An initial meeting took place in Dundee, where Professor James Hogg, Director of the University of Dundee White Top Research Unit was present and suggestions were made as to how INTACT, PAMIS and the White Top Unit could co-operate.

This was followed by a visit to the White Top Centre, run by the City of Dundee Social Work Department and the White Top Research Unit, which caters for people with profound and multiple impairments. The facilities available are very impressive and the emphasis on the abilities of the centre users and the importance of art and music among their activities is very marked, as is the commitment of the staff team.

INTACT attended two meetings with the PAMIS Parents' and Professionals' Consultative Group, where a number of parents volunteered to look at local museums and galleries from the point of view of intellectual access for their sons and daughters, and then reported back to the group. The findings were that, while there was still a lot to be done on physical access, many of this group had become more aware of the possibility of visiting such places as a leisure activity and that they would press museum/gallery staff for more sensory/tactile activities to be available.

Meantime, INTACT visited facilities run by Dundee City Council: the McManus Galleries, the Barrack Street Museum and the Central Library, Wellgate, when 'Inner Space', an exhibition including work done by White Top Centre users was showing. Verdant Works, a former jute mill managed by Dundee Heritage Trust, was also visited.

A later meeting was attended by representatives from PAMIS, Parveen Rodger of Dundee City Council Arts and Heritage Development Team, Professor James Hogg and INTACT. The discussion considered ideas for exhibitions which would appeal to people with very severe impairments. Parveen has an interest in community involvement and in working with disadvantaged groups as well as some experience of setting up the kind of multi-sensory display we had in mind. One possibility mentioned was a kind of interactive "discovering art" area with a title to encourage people of all ages and abilities to try it.

Something the White Top Centre staff were familiar with was a development of the "Snoezelen" sensory environment, based on the work of Lilli Neilson. They already had such a sensory environment within the centre where users could experience various sensations of touch, of sounds, of colour and light effects, and even smell, through aromatic oils. The ambience could be relaxing or stimulating, depending on the balance of sensations presented and users were able to express choice. The meeting thought it might be possible to adapt this idea to create an exhibition which would appeal to people with profound and multiple impairments, but also to the general public.

The White Top Centre users were already working, along with other community groups, on a textile project managed by Dundee Arts and Heritage for Dundee Heritage Trust's Verdant Works. When completed, this would be displayed at the McManus Galleries before the permanent installation at Verdant Works. They had also taken part in various ambitious drama productions where the centre users created costumes and scenery as well as being performers.

Other aspects of Access

- PAMIS and Professor James Hogg of the White Top Research Unit had an interest in the ideas for the new Dundee City Arts Centre, Dundee Contemporary Arts. This project had been awarded a major National Lottery Grant and was to be a partnership of three organisations, Dundee City Council, Dundee University and a new company, Dundee Contemporary Arts Limited. Professor Hogg was anxious to be included at an early stage to ensure that it would be fully accessible to people with profound and multiple impairments

- The application by Professor James Hogg to the Mental Health Foundation for funding under their *Promoting Choice for those with Severe, Profound or Multiple Disabilities* Initiative. This was to look at ways to encourage the expression of choice among the day centre users, increase their options, particularly in access to the arts, museums and exhibitions and monitor the results

- The request by PAMIS for an adult-sized changing bench to be provided in an accessible toilet in the new Museum of Scotland to enable people with severe and multiple impairments to be able to enjoy the collections in comfort

These added other strands to the work in Dundee, but they were closely interwoven with our original aims.

Dundee Contemporary Arts

INTACT attended a presentation in May 1997 at the White Top Centre. Professor Ian Howard, of Dundee University School of Fine Art, and Andrea Stark, Dundee City Council's Chief Arts Officer, both spoke. The new building would include:

- a centre for research in the arts (including workshops, artists-in-residence, publishing and multimedia), building on Dundee's international reputation for contemporary art

- two major galleries for touring exhibitions, a print workshop, space for education/interpretation, two cinema screens and film and TV workshops, activity rooms, seminar rooms, a restaurant and a huge café bar, possibly with live entertainment, as well as space for the necessary administration

- outreach work to different community groups, including those with special needs or with disabilities, those from ethnic minorities, and those with special interests.

The partnership providing this major cultural resource for the people of Dundee and surroundings is fully committed to access for all, as highlighted by the provision of an adult changing bench in one of the accessible toilets. Dundee Contemporary Arts, which will open in Autumn 1998, will have a bright, welcoming entrance to attract visitors. Once inside, they will be able to look at posters and leaflets, perhaps sit and have some refreshment, and be tempted by glimpses of activities or displays to venture further.

Dundee City Council's Arts and Heritage Department will have their headquarters within the new Arts Centre, and will provide support for the work of the Centre and manage some of the core facilities, including the two screen cinema. Arts and Heritage Management, Development, Arts Facilities, Marketing and Design and Administrative Services teams will all be based within the Centre.

Dundee University will run a Fine Art Research Centre from within the building. This will include an experimental gallery space, studios and facilities for post-graduate students and research fellows.

Dundee Contemporary Arts Ltd has responsibility for the programming of the two public gallery spaces and will run the printmakers' workshop and craft shop.

Mental Health Foundation Application

A meeting about an application to MHF for funding under their initiative *Promoting Choice for those with Severe, Profound or Multiple Disabilities* was held in Dundee in February. The organisations represented were:

Dundee City Council Arts and Heritage
Parveen Rodger, Development Team Leader

PAMIS
Loretto Lambe, Projects Director

White Top Centre, Dundee City Council Social Work Department
Lucy Rennie, Manager
Clare Hill, Speech and Language Therapist
Nigel Brodie, Development Officer

White Top Research Unit, Dundee University
Professor James Hogg, Director

INTACT
Ann Rayner, Project Officer

The proposal was that this network of contacts would explore ways in which adults with profound and multiple disabilities could better experience the sensory world and communicate their response to it. The development of special exhibitions which would provide both an outcome and a context for the work would be included, as would the encouragement of methods by which choice could be expressed, exercised and acted upon.

The enhancement of the intellectual accessibility of museum services would be part of this, with PAMIS, INTACT and the Dundee Arts and Heritage Service working together. The proposal was for a two year project in which to develop a number of contexts in which the response of the White Top Centre service users could be explored, monitored and evaluated and it was suggested that a part-time research assistant be appointed to liaise between the various parties, and implement observation and recording.
The immediate response to this was very discouraging as the application was not considered by the MHF as it emanated from Scotland, and the subsequent application to MHF Scotland (for £6,000, their limit) was rejected as *Choice* was not a funding priority for them.

However, in early 1998 it was announced that the initiative would be able to go ahead, thanks to a grant from *Children in Need* and that a Leisure Development Worker would be appointed to follow through some of the work of INTACT on access to museums and galleries as part of the remit of promoting a wider range of leisure activities. If possible, this Leisure Development Worker would make contact with INTACT before the end of the full-time Project.

The Adult Changing Bench for the Museum of Scotland

The initial request for this was made by the Tayside Co-ordinator of PAMIS, who pointed out that ...

... lack of suitable changing facilities is a problem which has been highlighted by parents and carers in our Group: it can completely put a stop to any plans they may have to take their daughters or sons out, with all the social isolation and lack of stimulation that implies for them, as well as the restriction it imposes on carers.

The National Museums of Scotland (NMS) was sympathetic to this request but there were some difficulties in installing such a facility as space had not been allowed for this in the original design for accessible

everyone became increasingly engaged in the work, anticipating what was about to happen, and a real group identity of those taking part in the project emerged.

toilets in the new building.

Alternative ways of accommodating this were investigated. As a result of these discussions, the issue was picked up by the NMS Disability Working Group on the grounds that the provision of an adult changing bench would meet the aims of the Trustees of NMS to make access to their collections as widely available as possible; it might help frail elderly visitors as well as those with quadriplegia and would comply with the Government's timetable for the implementation of the Disability Discrimination Act.

By early 1998 it was agreed to incorporate space for an adult changing bench in an area which would be accessible to wheelchair users. The facility, which will be an enormous advantage for people with multiple impairments or quadriplegia, will be located on the ground floor, adjacent to the main Tower Entrance on Chambers Street.

This will be an asset to the new Museum of Scotland and the adjoining Royal Museum which will enable them to cater for and attract visitors who might not otherwise be able to enjoy the collections. The NMS hopes to provide another similar facility when re-planning toilet accommodation for the Royal Museum. The Museum of Scottish Country Life at Wester Kittochside, set up by a partnership of NMS and NTS (National Trust for Scotland) and opening in 2001, will also provide an adult changing bench. This has been included in the plans from an early stage.

The fact that these facilities, which are by no means common, will be provided at several NMS sites sends out a strong signal about their commitment to the needs of people with disabilities and the importance placed on accommodating them.

Express Yourself Exhibition

At the same meeting in May 1997 which included the presentation about the Dundee City Arts Centre, delegates saw in progress the White Top multi-sensory "Installation" to be included in *Express Yourself* which would be opening at the Dundee City Council's McManus Galleries in June.

Express Yourself is a community art exhibition, initiated and managed by Dundee Arts and Heritage, exploring freedom of expression which had been inspired by the earlier *Freedom* exhibition at the same venue. This had been initiated by Amnesty International's Glasgow Group to celebrate freedom of expression. The groups who took part in 'Express Yourself' demonstrated a creative response to ideas such as the limits on personal freedom, inequality, discrimination, access and exclusion.

The varied artworks in this exhibition aimed to challenge stereotypes and explore different aspects of self-expression. Dundee Arts and Heritage enabled each group to work with a local artist to help them to realise their vision. Exhibits were produced in workshops which took place over several months, and included large banners with brightly printed collagraph prints created from highly textured collage blocks produced by the Dudhope Centre group.

The aims of the White Top contribution were:

- an end product that would be designed specifically to encourage each service user to explore and enjoy

- a method of making which would allow as much participation and fun as possible

The White Top installation consisted first of a large, inviting darkened 'box', about 200 x

200 x 200cm (big enough for a wheelchair user to enter), brightly painted on the outside and with heavy, printed curtains on the open side, but dark on the inside to reduce distractions. Elements that were specifically tailored to the needs of each service user had been created in the preceding workshops. These were intended to be used individually within the box but, for the purposes of the exhibition, several elements were exhibited within the box at once:

- participants were encouraged to push coloured net curtains with sparkly sequins aside and look at themselves in a mirror. To improve concentration lights around the mirror could be activated by a touch switch

- multi-coloured masks were created for a service user who enjoys looking at faces. To aid recognition one blank mask had slides of her family and friends projected on it that she could control

- one service user who constantly taps objects was encouraged to explore more slowly through the creation of a tactile tray with a series of fabric-covered foam tiles mounted on a board. Each one had different textures, colour contrasts and varying depths; some had fabric-covered loops joining one another and the positions of these could be varied

- the last exhibit was designed to encourage more controlled gestures, pointing as opposed to sweeping arm gestures and to improve verbal skills. There were three pairs of objects, interesting in themselves through colour and texture, but linked by association which was reinforced by simple touch switches called "Taction Pads" which 'spoke' a message or request when touched. This message, which could be varied by re-recording, referred to the other object of the pair, for example *"I am a little fish. Where is the big fish?"*

The White Top Box at *Express Yourself*

These different parts of the display were inspired by the interests of the centre users and created by them with help from staff at the White Top Centre and Community Arts workers. Obviously, given the group's problems of sight, grasp and reach, a lot of the help was 'hand over hand', but everyone became increasingly engaged in the work, anticipating what was about to happen, and a real group identity of those taking part in the project emerged.

Some increase in visual attention and enjoyment was noticed when two of the centre users were able to use long arm movements to apply paint, while others enjoyed the tactile exploration of both wet and dry "Mod-Roc" (quick setting plaster of Paris) while making the masks.

The work gave the service user opportunities to

- extend hand-to-eye co-ordination

- explore cause and effect, and ...

- … develop understanding and expression all ultimately leading to a greater control of the environment

The White Top Centre's aims appear to have been met in a highly satisfactory way. However there were a number of problems in displaying such work in an open gallery and the eventual effect of these was that some parts of the installation suffered damage.

From the point of view of Dundee Arts and Heritage staff, the main factors which resulted in this damage were:

- the piece was produced primarily as a learning tool for White Top Centre Service users and not as an exhibit for display in a public space

- the artists involved had not produced this kind of work before and did not appreciate how durable display solutions have to be

- some of the technical equipment was too sensitive to be used over a long period of time

However, despite the problems, they felt that the participation by the White Top Centre was extremely worthwhile. It broke new ground for them and they learnt a lot from having the piece on show as well as from colleagues at the Centre. They hope to incorporate lessons learnt in future displays.

INTACT had hoped to monitor some of the reactions of the public, and possibly of invited groups to the *Express Yourself* Exhibition, but this proved difficult until just before it closed and by then it had suffered the damage referred to. However, as well as being greatly impressed by the whole exhibition at its opening, we were able to encourage a number of people to visit it, including one from as far afield as Croydon, and we were able to see the wide range of comments in the visitors' book.

- I was very moved by this exhibition – especially the mirror.

- Art is about communication – significant here

- Unique exhibition compiled by unique and talented amazing people

Other ventures

INTACT provided a small amount of funding for materials for the White Top Centre's contribution to the *Elvis Lives* Exhibition in Glasgow. This was organised through the Project Ability Centre for Developmental Arts.

The White Top Centre and Dudhope Centre collaborated to make a life-sized Elvis figure, sprawled on a chair, looking at a TV set which showed a video of the workshops in action, and with a background screen with pictures of Elvis and graffiti. INTACT was able to see one of the workshops in progress and witness the participation of the centre users, and the intense concentration they showed while taking part in the creative process.

Elvis Lives was shown in various venues in Glasgow in January and February 1998, and included responses from artists from all over the world.

INTACT lent a "Talking Label" to Dundee Arts and Heritage for a trial. This equipment could provide an audio version of information for the benefit of people with learning difficulties, or those with a visual impairment, who might have a problem reading. As it could be moved from one display to another, and the message could easily be changed by re-recording, the museum staff found this a useful addition to displays which was liked by members of the public. During the temporary exhibition at Barrack Street Museum, – *and a bag full of Monkeys*, showing some of the collection of Professor Sir D'Arcy Thompson, it was used to give his 'voice' telling visitors about the objects. All the visitor had to do was "Press and Listen".

A short paper *Why Don't We Go to the Museum?* appeared in PMLD Link, a UK wide Bulletin for everyone working with people with profound and multiple learning difficulties, which is supported by Mencap City Foundation. This arose from INTACT's discussions with the PAMIS Parents' and Supporters' Group and was intended to raise awareness of the potential of visits to museums or galleries as possible activities for leisure or stimulation.

How far were the aims achieved?

1. Awareness has been raised among museum and gallery staff to the needs of people with profound and multiple impairments. Various ideas have been discussed, such as increasing the number of handling objects available in the museum, having handling objects on short-term loan to the White Top Centre, or the possibility of a sensory 'book' or some sort of collection of objects, audiotapes and even things to smell on a theme which could be used with people with PMLD to help them relate to museum objects or works of art. Unfortunately, despite there being no shortage of ideas, it has not so far been possible to put any of them into practice. This may well happen with the appointment of a Leisure Development Worker.

2. Though contacts existed earlier between staff in Dundee Arts and Heritage and staff and service users from the White Top Centre and from PAMIS, there are now more, for example with Andrea Stark, Chief Arts Officer, responsible for the establishment of Dundee Contemporary Arts, and with Anna Robertson through the 'Express Yourself' exhibition at the McManus Galleries in the summer of 1997. It seems likely that these contacts will continue to the benefit of both.

3. From being primarily concerned with physical access, parents and carers of people with PMLD are now much more aware of the need for intellectual access in addition to physical access in museums and galleries. We hope that they will continue to press for this and that, as the need becomes more widely recognised, more interactive and tactile opportunities will be offered.

4. Now that it is aware of the need, the National Museums of Scotland is installing adult changing benches at a number of its sites for the benefit of people with severe impairments. As Dundee Contemporary Arts will also have this facility, we hope that the need is becoming more widely recognised and that such provision will become standard.

Note

The "Talking Label" tried out at Dundee was supplied by Horizon Marketing of Huddersfield.

Awareness has been raised among museum and gallery staff to the needs of people with profound and multiple impairments.

From being primarily concerned with physical access, parents and carers of people with PMLD are now much more aware of the need for intellectual access in addition to physical access in museums and galleries.

If you are positive and welcoming in your approach and provide a good service, you will attract not only disabled customers but also their friends, relatives, carers and colleagues.

Access for people with disabilities has been on the agenda of museums and galleries for some time. The passing of the Disability Discrimination Act of 1995 has now made this a statutory duty and, moreover, makes the point that disability is not just about ramps, wide doorways and accessible toilets. Under "Who is disabled?", the Act specifically mentions *"someone who has a learning disability"* and *"someone who has significantly impaired speech"*.

Museum professionals are now realising that fully accessible facilities and exhibitions are making museums safer, more comfortable, and more meaningful for everyone. Ramps and elevators reduce accidents and accommodate baby carriages. Large print labelling with good contrast is meant to accommodate everyone. Captioned film and video heighten reading skills for children and foreign visitors; and exhibits presented at a height accessible to those who use wheelchairs are appreciated by adults of short stature and children as well.
The Accessible Museum Foreword by Daphne Wood Murray[1]

This conviction that improving access for people with disabilities, including learning and communication disabilities, helps many of the general public is endorsed by British authorities on museum access such as Caroline Keene and Rebecca McGinnis.
It also means that implementing these recommendations affects a wider section of the museum audience than might appear, which in turn suggests that money spent to improve access in general is beneficial in marketing and material terms, as well as being a legal requirement.

The leaflet 'What Service providers need to know' about the DDA[2] says on page 6 under *What's in it for me?*

There are a large number of disabled customers in the population and they choose where to spend their money. If you are positive and welcoming in your approach and provide a good service, you will attract not only disabled customers but also their friends, relatives, carers and colleagues. Word will soon get around that you are positive about disability.

Following naturally from this is the need for training in disability awareness across the whole spectrum of people who work in museums. Until everyone from senior management to attendants, shop and café staff and volunteer guides are aware of the needs of people with disabilities, the present, rather piecemeal, system will continue.

Eilean Hooper-Greenhill recognised this in *Museum and Gallery Education*[3] where she said:

Although in practice it is frequently staff concerned with education that tend to work with people with disabilities, it cannot be stressed too strongly that this is a cross-museum issue and of crucial importance to all museum staff, including designers, warding staff and management.

Without management to give a lead, disability issues will continue to be seen as an 'add on'. This can sometimes lead to greater expense when a disability consultant is brought in later and finds that things have to be altered to comply with existing legislation or, worse, if a disabled person has to point out a problem. If management is aware of the access needs of people with disabilities, physical, sensory or cognitive, then these needs can be addressed at an early stage of planning. This is true whether it is a new building, an extension, a new gallery, a refurbishment, or a temporary display that is being considered.

With this lead, designers, curators and education staff, all of whom should be aware of access issues, will be able from the beginning to incorporate features to help those with disabilities. This should avoid situations where the colour contrast on information panels is insufficient for those with visual impairments, or where a computer screen is fixed in a position which prevents a wheelchair user from reaching it.

Although professional disability awareness training is not cheap, there may well be longer-term cost benefits through avoiding the kind of pitfalls mentioned above and through the improvements which will be felt by the general public. Another possibility, alongside more formal training, is mentioned by Anne Tynan in a recent article *Open the Door*[4]. She makes the case for an integrated disability training programme which uses the knowledge and experience which many members of staff will have about disability matters and for developing informal contacts with people with disabilities.

What has been learnt from this research?

Much work is already being done in museums, galleries and historic buildings across the UK, and in other countries, to improve access for people with learning and communication disabilities. However, this is often the result of developments designed to improve access for people with other disabilities, particularly people with impaired vision, or to encourage more visitors from a wider social background and from ethnic minorities.

INTACT would like the specific needs of people with learning or communication disabilities to be recognised and catered for. We hope that this report comes at a time when museums and galleries, and their governing bodies, are becoming more aware of these needs and that it will encourage them to put some of the ideas in it into action.

We are all too well aware of the recent problems in funding faced by many museums whether national, local authority or privately run. However, since the passing of the DDA, improving access is not an optional extra, it is a statutory duty.

The INTACT research demonstrates what is widely recognised by many access authorities – that improvements in access for people with learning or communication disabilities, along with provision for those with other disabilities, helps all visitors. Museums are already competing with other attractions for visitors, and local authority museums are in competition for funding with other public services such as libraries and sports centres. At a time when visitor numbers are so critical to survival, such improvements could be vital.

Some examples of changes already being made are:

- to displays to make them more lively and attractive
- to attendants' uniforms to make them seem less intimidating – for example by dressing them in sweatshirts
- to the building by hanging up banners and providing more seating to make it more welcoming

Though these changes could be seen as just cosmetic, they usually also reflect a change in attitude which is demonstrated by many new or temporary exhibitions with a popular approach or theme. Examples taken from London MAG April/May 1998 include *The Power of the Poster* at the Victoria and

... implementing these recommendations affects a wider section of the museum audience than might appear ...

The strength of museums, art galleries and historic sites is the authenticity of the objects, works of art and buildings they look after. We must not be so dazzled by the use of interactive media that we forget the purpose of the message.

Albert Museum, *Myths and Monsters* at the Natural History Museum and *Hammer Horror* at the Museum of the Moving Image.

As displays are brought up to date, more varied interpretation methods are being introduced in many museums and galleries in order to appeal to a wider audience. On the whole these will benefit people with learning disabilities, and others who have problems with reading, by reducing the reliance on written material, and providing different ways to access an exhibit through audio, visual and tactile media.

However, there must be a balance. It is possible to go too far down the 'all things to all people' route and this can detract from the experience of seeing the actual objects in the collection. The strength of museums, art galleries and historic sites is the authenticity of the objects, works of art and buildings they look after.[5] We must not be so dazzled by the use of interactive media that we forget the purpose of the message. Interpretation is not an end in itself.

This report has emphasised that objects, potentially, can be made accessible to everyone. Because of this, museums are particularly suitable places for people with learning disabilities to learn and broaden their experience. People remember seeing an authentic object, still more if they have been able to handle it. Handling sessions at the Royal Museum in Edinburgh have demonstrated the fascination that real objects have for people with learning disabilities. They will remember holding a 500 million year old fossil trilobite, or an amulet which came from the wrappings of an Egyptian mummy, or feeling the weight of a Victorian flat iron which had to be heated by the fire and realising how different it would be to use from a modern electric steam iron.

Even where objects or works of art cannot be handled, they can still make an impression by virtue of their intrinsic beauty, interest or significance. Reproductions or virtual art galleries on CD-Rom are no substitute for actually seeing a work like Rembrandt's *Night Watch*, the actual jewellery worn by Mary, Queen of Scots, or for visiting a historic site such as the Tower of London. These are experiences that will be remembered because of the awe, fascination and sense of participation felt by the visitor.

Michael Cassin in *Heard but not seen … a new approach to outreach in the National Galleries of Scotland*[6] says:

> … these responses need to be generated by dealing with real things: original paintings, sculpture, real shards of Roman pottery, real pieces of Jacobite memorabilia, real steam engines, etc, not reproductions.

It is the object, work of art or site that is important and any way of providing information about it should be subordinate to the object itself. However, developments in modern technology cannot be ignored. These have a place in helping museums to make their displays more accessible to a wider visitor audience or providing a service to those with a special interest through access to a database.

Lessons drawn from the pilot projects

The pilot projects attempted to show how far some of the ideas that had emerged in the research about making displays more accessible would actually work in practice. The opinions of people with learning disabilities and those who support them were sought on how displays could be improved and how information about the objects or works of art could be made easier to understand.

These views gave us a base from which to judge how far the work we did was successful. It was encouraging how far these comments reinforced, in the particular situations, the general points which had emerged from earlier consultations and from the literature.

One of the most important lessons from the pilot projects is the need for consultation. It would be relatively easy for a museum or gallery to pick up some of the ideas suggested in this report, for example, multi-sensory interpretation methods, and apply them to their displays. But the results would be less satisfactory than if they had consulted people with learning disabilities in local day centres or supported accommodation about their needs. This kind of contact can lead to further consultation and possibly to help in doing an audit on 'intellectual access'. It may help in attracting funding and sponsorship, and fulfils the need for consultation mentioned by Rebecca McGinnis in *The Disabling Society*.[7]

Each group of disabled people must be located and targeted carefully. This should be done by museums before they develop their programmes and facilities. Groups of disabled people should be consulted from the planning stage right through to the evaluation of the finished product.

If a museum or gallery has taken the trouble to invite people from local day centres or supported accommodation to look at the existing displays or facilities in their institution before updating them, the people consulted are far more likely to visit as they will know something of what to expect, some of the staff will be familiar and they will feel some 'ownership' of the improvements.

This leads to the next important lesson of the pilot projects, which is that **consulting people with learning disabilities takes time**. This was true across the whole process; from setting up meetings, which often depended on the availability of support staff and transport, to the fact that people with learning disabilities are not always used to being asked their opinions. They need to feel comfortable and accepted before they can do so, and need time to express themselves. This time factor can be a real problem because staff in museums and galleries are normally very busy people, as are support staff for people with learning disabilities. It is better to be prepared for this, rather than to start a consultation process expecting it to be completed in a short time.

INTACT had very positive feedback from a senior lecturer working in a further education college special needs department. She was one of the group of people concerned with learning disabilities who became informal advisers to INTACT and took part in the Galleries and Handling Objects Pilot Projects. She thanked INTACT for the opportunity to enrich the curriculum and widen the horizons of her students and judged that we had succeeded in:

- raising awareness of the educational opportunities that exist in museums and art galleries

- challenging them to be imaginative in their use of these opportunities

- encouraging the concept of working in partnership with museum staff

- enabling staff and students to become familiar with the use of museum and gallery resources

One of the most important lessons from the pilot projects is the need for consultation with people with learning disabilities.

To be truly welcoming places, museums must continually reassess and respond to the needs of all visitors and find ways of turning 'access for all' from a catch-phrase into part of everyday practice.[8]

References

1. *The Accessible Museum* Foreword by D Wood Murray, Deputy Chairman for Public Partnership **National Endowment for the Arts AAM** (1992)

2. *What Service providers need to know – The Disability Discrimination Act of 1995* Minister for Disabled People (October 1996)

3. *Museum and Gallery Education* E. Hooper-Greenhill **Leicester Museum Studies Series** (1991)

4. *Open the Door* A Tynan Museums Journal (January 1998)

5. See *The Representation of the Past – Museums and Heritage in the Post-modern World* K Walsh **Routledge** (1992) for a detailed account of the heritage industry

6. *Heard but not seen … a new approach to outreach in the National Galleries of Scotland* M. Cassin in *Object Lessons* edit S Mitchell **HMSO** (1996)

7. *The Disabling Society* R McGinnis Museums Journal (June 1994)

8. *Something to see, Something to do, Somewhere to sit* J Earnescliffe in Museum Practice 4 (1997)

RECOMMENDATIONS

As a result of the research and of what we have learnt from the pilot projects, we feel strongly that there is a need for a greater recognition of the rights of people with learning disabilities to visit museums and galleries. These visits should be encouraged by specific measures to make them more interesting and enjoyable.

The Museums and Galleries Commission's recommendations in their *Guidelines on Disability for Museums and Galleries in the United Kingdom* (1995 and 1997) were referred to in the section *Preparing the Way* and these have informed our own suggestions.

Those we quoted then were:

- the need for a written policy and the drawing up of an action plan on access for people with disabilities

- the requirement for all staff, including members of the governing body, to have an understanding of disability issues and have training to ensure that they understand their responsibilities in fulfilling the policy

- the need to provide alternative or supplementary means of presentation to provide access to the collections and to facilities

- the recommendation that museums should develop links with community groups to promote initiatives that would benefit people with disabilities

INTACT Recommendations

We have separated these into three groups, recognising the different roles each can play in addressing the issues we have raised.

For funding bodies

- that priority for grant-aid is given to museums, galleries or historic sites which have in place, or are working towards, a policy or code of practice for the widest possible access of all kinds and recognising the principles outlined in the Scottish Office Education and Industry Department's Code of Practice referred to in the Introduction

For museums, galleries, historic sites and all service providers

- that they should have an access policy which refers specifically to intellectual access and which recognises the needs of people with learning or communication disabilities alongside those of people with other disabilities

- that, as a result of this policy, they should authorise an access audit exercise which embraces the building, the collection, the services and the publicity materials

- that all museum, gallery or historic site staff should be made aware of the needs of people with learning disabilities through disability awareness training and that this should be an essential part of the training of all staff at whatever level from attendants to director. This should include:

– help and advice for front of house staff in making visitors with learning disabilities welcome and in assisting them if problems arise

– encouraging education staff to include people with learning disabilities in the programmes or workshops they devise

– making curators and designers aware of the needs of people with learning disabilities when planning exhibitions or updating existing displays

– making directors, governors and trustees of museums, who are responsible for policy decisions, aware of the needs of people with learning disabilities alongside those of people with other disabilities so that corporate plans and policies and long-term planning can accommodate such requirements

- that links be established between museum and gallery staff on one hand and organisations for people with learning disabilities on the other:

– at the most basic level for museum staff, this could consist of sending out information about what is already provided and asking for comments

For organisations and facilities for people with learning disabilities

- through organisations such as People First, day/resource centres, colleges and supported accommodation, people with learning disabilities should make contact with their local museums and galleries to find out what facilities there are

- by putting forward their concerns, they may influence the design of new displays, press for improvements in signage and even take part in training staff in awareness of their problems

The essential feature of these recommendations is that everyone – funders, service providers and users – should be working together. By doing this, museum/gallery staff and people with learning disabilities along with those who support them can jointly explore the most appropriate ways of making their distinctive collections accessible.

The essential feature of these recommendations is that everyone – funders, service providers and users – should be working together.

BOOKS

Aldridge, D
Principles of Countryside Interpretation and Interpretive Planning Countryside Commission for Scotland HMSO (1975)

Allan, J et al
The Challenge of Age Glasgow School of Art (1996)

Anderson, D
A Common Wealth – Museums and Learning in the United Kingdom Department of National Heritage (1997)

Ambrose, T
edit *Working with Museums* SMC (1988)
Education in Museums, Museums in Education HMSO (1987)

American Association of Museums
The Accessible Museum (1992)

Association of Scottish Visitor Attractions
Interpretation – A Guide ASVA

Basic Skills Agency
Making Reading Easier (1992)

Buckinghamshire County Museum
A Touch of Bucks – a Guide for People with Learning Difficulties Aylesbury (1997)

Brechin, A and Walmsley, J
edit *Making Connections – Reflecting on the lives and experiences of People with Learning Difficulties* Hodder and Stoughton/Open University (1989)

BT Countryside for All
A Good Practice Guide to Disabled People's Access to the Countryside The Fieldfare Trust (1997)

Carnegie Council Review
After Attenborough: Arts and Disabled People (1988)

Carnegie UK Trust
Arts and Disabled People – the Attenborough Report (1985)

Carter, J
A Sense of Place Tourism and Environment Initiative (1997)

Cayton, A C
Store Design – Recommendations for Improvement Institute of Grocery Distribution (1994)

Chadwick, A & Stannett, A
edit *Museums and the Education of Adults* NIACE (1995)

Cité des Sciences et de l'Industrie
Des visites confortables pour tous La Villette, Paris (1992)

Cox, M
A Short guide to Interpretation Scottish Arts Council Information Directory

Davidson, B
New Dimensions for traditional Dioramas: Multi-sensory Additions for Access, Interest and Learning Boston Museum of Science (1991)

Davidson, K
Learning with Objects Marischal Museum, University of Aberdeen (1994)

Denman, R and Clarkson, S
The Disabled Visitor English Tourist Board Insights (1991)

Department of Education and Science
Use of Museums in Adult and Community Education HMSO (1988)

Department of National Heritage/Culture Media and Sport
People taking Part (1996)

Direction des Musées de France
Des Musées pour Tous: manuel d'accessibilité physique et sensorielle des Musées (1994)

Director of Scottish Services
For A' the Folk Public Services Agency (1987)

Durbin, G
edit *Developing Museum Exhibitions for Lifelong Learning* GEM/Stationery Office (1996)

Durbin, Morris & Wilkinson
A Teacher's Guide to learning from Objects English Heritage (1990)

Earnescliffe, J
In through the front door The Arts Council of Great Britain (1992)

English Tourist Board
Tourism for All (1994)

Falk, J & Dierkind, L
The Museum Experience Whalesback Books (1994)

Fondation de France & ICOM
Museums without Barriers Routledge (1991)

Foster, L
Perspectives on Access to Museums and Art Galleries in Historic Buildings MGC (1996)

Gall, J
Access Prohibited? – Information for designers of public access terminals

Gammon, B and Moussouri, T
Text and Labels – How to make them readable
Science Museum, London, unpublished internal document, (October 1995)

Gardner, H
Frames of Mind: the theory of multiple intelligences Basic Books, New York (1983)

Gateshead Access Panel
Designing to Enable (1997)

Greeves, M & Martin, B
Chalk,Talk and Dinosaurs SMC & Moray House Publications (1993)

Gregory, W
The Informability Manual HMSO (1997)

Harland, J et al
Attitudes to Participation in the Arts Heritage, Broadcasting and Sport report for DNH and NFER (1995)

Holmes-Siedle, J
Barrier-free Design Butterworth Architecture (1996)

Hooper-Greenhill, E
Museums and the Shaping of Knowledge Routledge (1991) edit *Initiatives in Museum Education* University of Leicester (1989), *Writing a Museum education policy* University of Leicester (1991), *The Educational Role of the Museum* Routledge (1994), *Museum, Media and Message* Routledge (1995)

Humphries, S & Gordon P
Out of Sight Channel 4 (1992)

Kavanagh, G
edit *Museum Languages: Objects and Texts* Leicester University Press (1991)

Kently, E & Negus, D
Writing on the Wall National Maritime Museum, Greenwich (1989)

Lissargue, J
La Cité des Sciences et de l'Industrie Electa (1988)

London Museums Service, edit Trevelyan, V
Dingy Places with different kinds of bits (1991)

Loomis, R J
Museum Visitor Evaluation American Association for State & Local History (1987)

Lord, G
edit *The Arts and Disabilities* Carnegie UK Trust (1981)

Lothian Coalition of Disabled People
Guidelines for producing information in large print (1995)

McConkey, R
Who Cares? Community Involvement with Handicapped People Souvenir Press, London (1987)

Macdonald, A, Project co-ordinator
The Challenge of Age Glasgow School of Art, Foulis Press (1996)

MAGDA: *Disabled People Welcome* (1993)
Disability Design Museums (1988)
Opening the door to disabled people (1987)
Sharing the Wisdom of Age (with Age Concern) (1995)

Majewski, J
Accessible Exhibition Design Smithsonian Institution, Washington, (1996)
Part of your General Public is Disabled Smithsonian Institution, Washington (1987)

Maslow, A
Motivations and Personality Harper & Row, New York (1994)

Mencap
Welcoming customers with learning disabilities – a training pack (1996)

Mental Health Foundation
Building Expectations (1996)

Merriman, N
Beyond the Glass Case Leicester Museum Studies Series (1991)

Metropolitan Museum of Art
Standards Manual for Signs and Labels New York (draft) (1995)

Minister for Disabled People
Disability Discrimination Act Information Pack (1996)
The Disability Discrimination Act – What Service Providers need to know (1996)
A brief guide to the Disability Discrimination Act for people with learning disabilities (1995)

Museums and Galleries Commission
Disability Resource Directory for Museums (1993) and *Supplement* (1997)
Guidelines on Disability for Museums and Galleries in the United Kingdom (1992) updated as: *Access to Museums and Galleries for People with Disabilities* (1997)
Ours for Keeps: resource pack for raising awareness of Conservation and Collection Care (1997)
Perspectives on Access to Museums and Galleries in Historic Buildings (1996) Foster, L and Coles, A, edit

Mitchell, S
edit *Object lessons: the role of Museums in Education* HMSO (1996)

National Foundation for Educational Research
Attitudes to Participation in the Arts Department of Heritage, Broadcasting & Sport (1996)

National Information Forum
How to provide information well (1996)

Nisbet, P and Poon, P
Special access technology CALL (Communication Aids for Language and Learning) Centre, University of Edinburgh (1998)

Nolan, G
Designing Exhibitions to include People with Disabilities NMS (1997)

Northamptonshire County Council
Pathways to partnership (1995)

Open University
Workbook 2 for K668 (1990)

Pearce, S
edit *Objects of Knowledge* Athlone (1990), *Art in Museums* Athlone (1995)

Pearson, A and Aloysius, C
Museums and children with learning difficulties: The Big Foot British Museum (1994)

Pearson, A
Arts for Everyone Carnegie UK Trust (1985)

People First
Access First – a guide on how to give written information for people with learning difficulties (1997)

People First, Scotland
Special schools – and now we are different (1996)

Plain English Campaign
How to Write Reports in Plain English Manchester (1995)

Reinwardt Studies in Museology No 1
Exhibition Design as an Educational Tool Reinwardt Academy, Leiden, Netherlands (1983)

RNIB/MAGDA
Talking Touch Seminar Report, (Kirby, Sullivan, Corvest etc) (1988)

RNIB
Discovering Museums HMSO (1993)
Making Museums Accessible (1995)
Building Sight London, HMSO

Royal Ontario Museum
Hands On ROM (1979)

Sassoon, R & Gaur, A
Signs, Symbols and Icons Intellect Books (1997)

Scottish Museums Council
Museums are for People SMC (1985)

Scottish Natural Heritage
Provoke, Relate, Reveal – a policy framework for interpretation SNH, Battleby, Redgorton, Perth (1997)

Scottish Office Education and Industry Department
A Parent's guide to Special Educational Needs (1993)
Provision made by the Community Education Service in Fife for people with special needs (1996)

Scottish Tourist Board
Site interpretation: A Practical Guide STB (1993)

Scottish Working Group on Information Services for People with Disabilities
Enabling Information (1995)

Serrell, B
Exhibit Labels – an Interpretive Approach Altamira (1996)

Smithsonian Institution Guidelines
Accessible Exhibition Design Washington (1997)

Springer, S and Deutsch, G
Left Brain, Right Brain Freeman (1993)

Steiner, C K
Help for the Special Educator Metropolitan Museum of Art, New York (1981)
Museums and the Disabled Metropolitan Museum of Art, New York (1979)
Museum Education for Retarded Adults: reaching a neglected audience Metropolitan Museum of Art, New York (1981)

Sudbury, P & Russell, T
Evaluation of Museum and Gallery Displays Liverpool University Press (1995)

Talboys, G K
Using Museums as an Educational Resource Arena (1996)

Tilden, F
Interpreting Our Heritage University of North Carolina Press (1957)

Tynan, A
Adventures in Disability Tynan Publishing (1997)

Tyne & Wear Museums
Guidelines for Printed Information

Vanier, J
The Challenge of L'Arche Longman and Todd, London (1982)

Veverka, J
Interpretive Master Planning Falcon Press, Montana (1994)

Walsh, K
The Representation of the Past – Museums and Heritage in the post-modern world Routledge (1992)

Wolfensberger, W
The Principle of Normalisation in Human Services Toronto (1972)

Articles and Papers

Anderson, D
Time to jump into the learning loop Museums Journal 11 (1997)
Beyond Museums: objects and cultures Journal for Education in Museums 13 (1992)
Gradgrind driving Queen Mab's Chariot: What Museums have (and have not) learnt from Adult Education in *Museums and the Education of Adults* edit Chadwick and Stannett, NIACE (1995)
Museums must recognise the needs of all users Adults Learning 8, 7, NIACE (1997)

Arts Council of England
Guidelines for Marketing to Disabled People (1993)

Artymowski, J D
Services for the mentally handicapped at the Royal Castle, Warsaw in *Museums without Barriers* ICOM (1991)

Aven, L
The work of the Commission on the Disabled at the Cité des Sciences et de l'Industrie and the Charter for the Disabled in *Museums without Barriers* ICOM (1991)

Bennett, S
Museum Education and Information Technology in *Initiatives in Museum Education* edit E Hooper-Greenhill, University of Leicester Department of Museum Studies (1989)

Bicknell, S and Mann, P
A Picture of Visitors for Exhibition Developers (1993) reprinted in *Developing Museum Exhibitions for Lifelong Learning* edit G Durbin, GEM/Stationery Office (1997)

Bitgood, S
Visitor Orientation and Circulation:some general Principles (1992) reprinted in *Developing Museum Exhibitions for Lifelong Learning* edit G Durbin, GEM/Stationery Office (1996)

Bown, L
An Adult Educator's Perspective in *Museums and the Education of Adults* edit Chadwick & Stannett, NIACE (1995)

Burda, P
Something for everyone Museum News (Nov/Dec 9) Boston Science Museum

CALL Centre
Alternatives to the Standard Keyboard CALL Information Sheet 2, Communication Aids for Language and Learning, University of Edinburgh (1994)

Canadian Museums Association
Reading the Museum/Lire le Musée (1995 – 6)

Carnegie, E
Case Study: Working with Women's Groups reprinted in *Developing Museum Exhibitions for Lifelong Learning* edit G Durbin GEM/Stationery Office (1996)

Carter, J
*How **old** is this text?* Environmental Interpretation (Feb 1993)

Cassin, M
Are you having a nice time? in *Object Lessons* edit S Mitchell, HMSO (1996)

Churcher, I
Guidelines for Effective Museum Leaflets, MA Thesis, University of Leicester (1995) unpublished

Clutten, S
The Buck starts here Museums Journal (January 1996)

Coles, A
Disability on the Agenda in *Museums in Britain* (Summer 1996)

Conybeare, C
Access Advisers: Nottingham Castle Museum and Art Gallery Museum Practice 4 (1997)

Coxall, H
Issues of Museum Text (1991) reprinted in *Developing Museum Exhibitions for Lifelong Learning* edit G Durbin GEM/Stationery Office (1996)
Writing for different audiences (1991) reprinted in *Developing Museum Exhibitions for Lifelong Learning* edit G Durbin, GEM/Stationery Office (1996)

Curtis, N
Touching the Past GEM News

Davidson, B et al
Increased Exhibit Accessibility through multi-sensory interaction in *The Educational Role of the Museum* edit E Hooper-Greenhill, Routledge (1994)
New England Lifezones in the Museum of Science, Boston in *The Accessible Museum* AMA (1992)

Davis, P
Underwater Overview Museums Journal (February 1992)

Dean, D
Permission to stick on labels Museums Journal (July 1996)

Dobinsky, L
Museums and Literacy: a natural partnership Journal of Education in Museums, No 18 (1997)

Dodd, J
Museums for All? GEM News 50
What information do you need? GEM News 55
Whose museum is it anyway? Journal for Education in Museums

Earnescliffe, J
Something to see, Something to do, Somewhere to sit Museum Practice 4 (1997)

Edwards, N
Learning without walls in *Adults Learning* 8.7 (1997)

Esteve-Coll, E
A Yearning for Learning Museums Journal (March 1993)

Falconer, H
Bucking the bad luck story Museums Journal (January 1996)

Falk, J
The use of time as a measure of visitor behaviour and exhibit effectiveness Roundtable Reports 7 (4) (1982)

Giusti, E
Visitors Evaluate the Evolution Hall Exhibitionist (Fall 94)

GEM Training Day Report
Research into Learning in Museums GEM News, 62 (Summer 1996)

Green, V
The Access to Image Project GEM 14 (1993)

Hall, L
Opening Glass Cases GEM News, 50
People and Places GEM News, 61

Hein, G
Evaluating a Display adapted for People with Learning Difficulties ECSITE Newsletter (Aug/Sept 1990)

Heumann Gurian, E
Noodling around with Exhibition Opportunities reprinted in *Developing Museum Exhibitions for Lifelong Learning* edit G Durbin, GEM/Stationery Office (1996)

Hinton, M
Handling Collections: a whole museum issue Journal for Education in Museums 14 (1993)

Hirschi, K D and Scriven, C
Effects of Questions on Visitor Reading Behaviour (1988) reprinted in *Developing Museum Exhibitions for Lifelong Learning* edit G Durbin, GEM/Stationery Office (1996)

Historic Scotland
Access to the Built Heritage (1996)

Hood, M S
Staying away – why people choose not to visit museums Museum News (April 1983)

Hooper-Greenhill, E
A *Museum Educator's Perspective* in *Museums and the Education of Adults* edit Chadwick & Stannett, NIACE (1995)
Audiences – a cultural Dilemma in *Art* in *the Museum* edit S Pearce, Athlone (1995)
Museums in Education in *Working with Museums* edit T Ambrose, SMC (1988)

Horowitz, S
Maintaining your exhibits ... and your Visitors in *Exhibitionist* (Fall 95)

Jones, D
The Adult Learner in *Museums and the Education of Adults* edit Chadwick & Stannett, NIACE (1995)

Kelly, J
Picture This, Museums Journal (July 1996)

Kirby, W
Access to Museums by Adult Learners with Disabilities in *Museums and the Education of Adults* edit Chadwick and Stannett, NIACE (1995)

Lister, D
Are museums turning Britain into a heritage Disneyland? The Independent (20/5/97)

MAGDA, London
Access to Information Minutes of Meeting at the British Museum (June 1997)

McGinnis, R
The DDA: Duty or Opportunity? Museum Practice 5 (1997)
Making sense of Art paper presented at the Fruitmarket Gallery Interpretation Seminar in November 1996
edit *The Disabling Society* Museums Journal (June 1994)

McLean, K
Computers in Exhibits: what are they good for? Curator 35 (1992)

McManus, P
Label Reading Behaviour (1989) reprinted in *Developing Museum Exhibitions for Lifelong Learning* edit G Durbin GEM/Stationery Office (1996)

Marwick, S
Upstairs, Downstairs at Lauriston Castle in 1903 Scottish Museum News 8,4 (1992)

Moffat, H
A Common Wealth in *Adults Learning* 8.7 (1997)

Moore, K
Open House, Open Mind Museums Journal (March 1993)

Musées, No 214
Recevoir les handicapés (1997)

Nicholson, R
Smith goes Green Museums Journal (September 1990)

Ouertani, N
A Scheme for mentally handicapped children in Tunisia Muséum, Paris, UNESCO Vol 33 no 3 (1981)

Pearson, A
The Vicious Circle; Museum education and some handicapped people in some London Museums Journal for Education in Museums (1982)
Museum Education and Disability in *Initiatives in Museum Education* edit E Hooper-Greenhill, University of Leicester Dept of Museum Studies (1989)
Touch exhibitions in the United Kingdom in *Museums without Barriers,* ICOM (1985)

Pitman, J
The Exhibitionists The Times (5/4/97)

Prochak, M
Multimedia is the message Museums Journal (May 1990)

Reising, G
The National Museum of Fine Arts in Karlsruhe, Germany in *Museums without Barriers* ICOM (1991)

Roberts, L C
Educators on Exhibition Teams: a New Role, a New Era Journal of Museum Education (Fall 1994)

Serrell, B and Raphling, B
Computers on the Exhibition Floor (1992) reprinted in *Developing Museum Exhibitions for Lifelong Learning* edit G Durbin GEM/Stationery Office (1996)

Scaife, S
Access Project at Wakefield Art Gallery Museums Journal (January 1996)
Welcoming adults with learning difficulties at Wakefield Museums and Galleries in *Museums and the Education of Adults* edit Chadwick and Stannett, NIACE (1995)

Spalding, J
Communicating Generously Museums Journal (February 1992)

Stannett, A
The Adult Visitor Journal for Education in Museums 14 (1993)

Swift, F
Time to go Interactive? Museum Practice 4 (1997)

Thompson, C
The Accessible Museum Museums Visitor (1997)

Tynan, A
Let me show you Case Study in *Object Lessons* edit S Mitchell, SMC/HMSO (1996)
Open the Door Museums Journal (Jan 1998)

Watson, R
Eureka GEM News

Wear, D
Training and Staff Development in *Museums and the Education of Adults* edit Chadwick and Stannett, NIACE (1995)

Westerland, S & Knuthammar, T
Creative work among the mentally handicapped Muséum, Paris, UNESCO Vol 33 no 3 (1981)

Wood, R
Museum Learning: a family focus Journal for Education in Museums 11 (1990) reprinted in *Developing Museum Exhibitions for Lifelong Learning* edit G Durbin GEM/Stationery Office (1996)
Museums, Means and Motivation: Adult Learning in a Family Context in *Museums and the Education of Adults* edit Chadwick and Stannett, NIACE (1995)